ARCADE FIRE
BEHIND THE BLACK MIRROR

ARCADE FIRE
BEHIND THE BLACK MIRROR
MICK MIDDLES

OMNIBUS PRESS
London / New York / Paris / Sydney / Copenhagen / Berlin / Madrid / Tokyo

Contents

Introduction

Who The Fuck Is Arcade Fire?

"I AV NO CLU WHO THE SUBURBS IS. WHY THEY GET FICK AWARD WHEN GAGA THERE. THEY PLAY N NON OF MY PEOPLE KNOWS WHO THEY ARE. NOBIDY LIKE EM"

"FUCK YOU? Who the fuck is Arcade Fire? Stop riggin this shit. U lost many viewers. Look at the reactions. You lost a lot"
(Messages on 'whoisarcadefire.com' website)

It was an awards ceremony like no other, but in many ways it was like *all* the others.

It is February 2011 and we are in Las Vegas amid a swirling mess of joyless sycophancy, excitable chatter, insincere smiles and the nervous undertone of cautious expectation. Scan the crowd and gasp at famous faces, all primed to bask their egos in shameless glory. They peer over vast, round, drinks-laden tables, a veritable orgy of smug celebrity, the full blast of paparazzi flash, all languishing in tabloid cheese. Baby-faced, miniskirted female television presenters prowl freely.

And look at those faces: Justin Bieber, Eminem and, of course, the omnipresence of Lady Gaga and her not-really-that-strange kookiness. All of them are surrounded by bobbing and swaying minions; important looking men trying desperately to look even more important and glancing nervously towards the stage. The mind loses track of reality as gong after gong is presented between stilted, scripted announcements. Everything, it seems, is clipped to a perfect choreography. The thoroughly stage-managed slice of contemporary music is spliced with glittery glances of stars of yesteryear, all here to play tribute – and gain kudos by association – with the fast rising stars of 2011.

Perhaps due to the growing realisation that the record industry is on its knees in subjection to file sharing, this year's Grammys seems a little different. Record company nerves are more on edge than usual. A million sales can follow a Grammy, making that priceless CD sticker reading 'Grammy Award Winner' all the more important. In an age of universal uncertainty, with the entire music business shattered into fragments by digital downloads and the fast-moving listening habits of its audience, *any* chance of gong glory is no longer to be sniffed at.

Sell Out?

"Of course. Fucking hope so, maan."

No longer is the concept of 'sell out' regarded with disdain. On the contrary, it is actively encouraged by companies and fans alike, even centrally placed in the marketing ethos of hip-hop and rap. Prestigious awards like the Brits and Grammys are merely a cog in this increasingly cynical game. Best Album equals best marketing too. People will keep their jobs. People will smile and, tonight, tumble into gleeful inebriation.

On this night, the honour of announcing the winner of the 'Best Album' category falls to Barbra Streisand, though even a star of such magnitude seems fazed when she rips open the envelope, her facial features noticeably contracting as a twinge of anxiety creeps in. She must not mess up this simple task. She mustn't… and she is squinting at the name before her. She is momentarily nonplussed, a flash of panic, of unrecognition, crossing her exquisitely powdered brow. What is the name on this card?

"And the winner is…"

She is visibly fumbling at this point, clearly distressed. Her mouth closes around two words… two words delivered in a state of questioning terror. Was it an announcement? Was it a question? Her eyes are shining with "What the fuck?"

"The winner is…Theeee Suuuubuuuuuurbs?"

For once there is an eerie lull. Then a lonely squeal. Then the sight of a small excitable huddle. Of Arcade Fire's Régine Chassagne spinning round in glee… and of an uncomfortable band lost in a state of collective embarrassment.

A chill ripples through the room, a low growl. Cameras flash on the less than exalted faces of disappointed superstars. Lady Gaga looks lost in thunderous disbelief. Elsewhere, there's a sense of embarrassment. Will someone get sacked for this, tomorrow? We expected to win that. Who the fuck is Arcade Fire?

A band with no hits, that's who it is. A band with no identifiable genre… which, in itself, makes them a dangerous property. A band rarely glimpsed on MTV. A band that looks like they don't belong anywhere, especially at the Grammys.

The band with no hits takes the stage and begins to play 'Month Of May', performing before stunned, silent, stony faces. Nil movement. The sheer energy of suppressed hate. Horrified faces…

Then they play a second song. This time it's 'Ready To Start' and, at last, there is noticeable crowd movement. An initial trickle has become an embarrassing stream aiming for the exit. It's a protest of apathy, setting the seal on a thoroughly disappointing evening.

I mean. Who the fuck is Arcade Fire?

"I thought it was hilarious… at the ceremony," Arcade Fire's Win Butler would later tell Q magazine's Simon Goddard. "I don't think we have ever played to a more apathetic audience in our lives."

The band flash rebellious faces on finishing, darting from the stage to the door, and Régine twice, three times, clashes with over-zealous security, their arms across the door. "You can't go back there, miss… miss… MISS. You cannot go back there. That is for artists only."

Eventually, and only after a series of phone calls, Régine is duly rescued from the ignominy of being the first Grammy-winning artist ever to be barred from her own awards ceremony. But, in another way, ejection from the ceremonial hall would have been perfect.

Régine: "It was kinda funny. I can see the funny side to that. And maybe a little symbolic too. I don't really know the truth of it. Maybe that security guy hadn't been briefed properly. Maybe he expected female musicians to look like Lady Gaga or something. Or maybe he was a Kings of Leon fan... I honestly don't know."

It may seem ironic, perverse in its stupidity perhaps, to object so much to an awards ceremony that you are moved to instigate a website dedicated to emphasising a band's state of obscurity. 'Who is Arcade Fire' even became lodged as a top five Google search that catapulted their name through the digital catacombs of Facebook and Twitter, virtually creating for themselves a new cult status among the Gaga freaks and light hip-hop tribes – the very people who objected in the first place. So powerful was this electronic wave, so penetrative the new media, that one might have been forgiven for thinking it a record company scam, Machiavellian/McLarenesque in its subversive effectiveness, Suddenly the band with no hits, the band plucked from dense obscurity at the Grammy ceremony, were gathering pace. Could this really have happened by accident?

Win Butler: "I can understand why people might think that such a thing would be instigated by some scheming management but I can only assure people that it wasn't the case. I might have been proud of it, if it had been. How strange to be at the centre of some kind of scandal without actually doing anything outrageous. It's hardly the Sex Pistols, is it? Must admit, I did think the whole thing was really funny."

In *Q* magazine, again, Simon Goddard wondered if this was true when Win saw the internet message claiming victory for Kings Of Leon, and calling Arcade Fire "faggots".

Butler: "Um, I didn't get too deep down on the comments because, really, it is the lowest of the low form of communication. Hmmm."

More perverse, perhaps? The sight of a full page ad in the *New York Times*, costing New York-based marketing executive Steve Stoute £40,000 to promote that increasingly tired notion that receiving their Grammy between songs during the ceremony's closing credits was evidence enough of the music industry's 'wayward marketing exercises', the inference being that it takes an expert to notice such a blatant marketing scam, or an expert to be fooled by the sheer chance of it all.

The charge of unworthy obscurity had already worn redundant... it wasn't as if this award was given to some upstart band enjoying a flash-in-the-pan hit album, either.

By the time of the awards ceremony Arcade Fiore had three American number one albums already under their belt. Tickets for the American leg of their world tour wére already shifting heavily, 30,000 over three days in Chicago alone while, over in England, advance sales for their biggest single headline date – the biggest and most prestigious show of their career, at London's Hyde Park, in June – zipped from Ticketmaster's website with unprecedented speed. And this despite the gig taking place right in the heart of the British festival season, just one week after Glastonbury and during the same weekend as the highly favoured Hop Farm event in Surrey.

But it was Arcade Fire who would be the band to see in 2011 as, indeed, they had been for a full five years. Arguably – and it *is* arguable – the largest band in the world. If not so, then certainly the most intriguing and, as the *NME* noisily proclaimed, 'The most exciting live act on the planet.'

But... who the fuck?

Dismiss that as crude, ignorant, naïve, juvenile or blandly streetwise, if you will, the fact remains that it is not a bad question. Especially to the eyes and ears of those – mid-teens to mid-twenties, perhaps? – whose musical and cultural advancement has been through the gloopy soup of contemporary R'n'B and the mainstream fringe of rap. I wouldn't be openly dismissive of this ocean-sized genre, to be honest – Kanye West, Jay Z have both permeated the rockist wall of my listening habits, for what it's worth – but, in league with the digital age, the visual effect has been to diminish instrumentation. Music, as such, appears as soundtracks to soft porn videos where rappers and scantily clad ladies frolic on beaches, in cars and bars, even on stage in some vast arena. The only noticeable instrumentation is often reduced to the sight of a spangly mic, as much worn as used; a shimmering item of bling and status. Generally speaking, award-winning males are elegantly black-suited and visually cruising. The females are mesmerisingly famous and iconic, shining beacons of elegance and poise. You know their names. We all suffer their omnipresence as the power of their influence filters down through to the crass global mimicry of *X Factor* ad infinitum.

This sanitised cultural arena offers nothing remotely like Arcade Fire, and even the competing and giant arena of rock and its myriad genres seems firmly slammed in reverse, amplifying the echoes of Black Sabbath or Neil Young or The Velvet Underground. Only in the recent emergence of Americana, which itself kicks back strongly to The Band and Grateful Dead, will you nudge within a country mile of anything remotely like Arcade Fire in terms of visuals, sound, lyrics, attitude and appeal.

But to the global audience of an awards show... who, indeed, the fuck are Arcade Fire? Just look at this lot. There are seven of them – sometimes more, but that is not the issue here – an awkward, ill-fitting seven at that, of all shapes and sizes, it seems; for English viewers a grown-up Bash Street Kids, none of whom assume the accepted traits of 'contemporary icon' or even attract attention in the accepted manner. The central husband and wife team, Win Butler and Régine Chassagne, seem oddly configured, awkward. He's very tall and she's quite small. Régine, petite and blessed with an increasingly commanding presence, is unquestionably attractive but her looks don't conform to the pop star prototype. Win is lanky, powerful, passionate and looks ever-so-slightly uncomfortable. Beyond them is diminutive Sarah Neufeld, standing aside, openly mouthing the words while her arm slices across a violin. Alongside are Tim Kingsbury, Will Butler, Richard Reed Parry and Jeremy Gara. In an age and an arena where guitar, bass, drums and keyboards are regarded as fading tools of ancient lore – 'dad rock' accoutrements to use a particularly derogative label – what exactly is happening here? What are these people playing at on their guitars, drums, bass, piano, violin, viola, cello, double bass, xylophone, side-drum, French horn, flugelhorn, accordion, hurdy gurdy, harp and mandolin. One can only imagine the astonished and dismissive face of, say, Simon Cowell should such a dishevelled and unconventional troupe have the temerity to audition before him, or before a rigidly controlling global television regime that prefers its females to launch into a Mariah Carey warble or Shakira come-on, and its boy bands to perform a step-perfect dance-troupe formation routine.

And that is just the start. Those who so vociferously complained about Arcade Fire's victory are unlikely to dig too deeply into either the bizarrely baroque music they play or, indeed, the lyrics that, at once, evoke the past and present... and, furthermore, appear to be launched from some oddball Gnostic heart. This is the sound of an ancient church, full of shadows and light, mystery and paranoia, dragged from a muse built from both academic immersion, the mysteries of childhood and, here is the twist, an unlikely eye for the futuristic. Generally speaking, this is not subject matter found in singles by Katy Perry, Avril Lavigne or Jay Z.

You would have to squint hard towards, say, the now existential and gloriously aloof figure of Tom Waits to find anything closely comparable to Arcade Fire; artists who, despite being accepted into the Rock'n'Roll Hall of Fame (whatever that is) rarely find themselves invited to a televised music awards ceremony. Arcade Fire construct their music with unconventional flare. Even many of the British indie bands who flicker in their influences – of which much more, later – did not and do not tread such mainstream boards with such bravado.

Who are they, indeed, this strange band that is getting stranger, despite moving deeply into the mainstream with their third album? There, indeed, lies a whole mess of paradox and contradiction. They are a band that flies between the black and the white. They speak in tongues.

At the time of that awards ceremony, despite a worldwide presence that had been increasing in focus since the launch of their first album, *Funeral*, in 2004 (2005 in the UK, thanks to Rough Trade), they were a hit band with no hit singles, though in reality they were no strangers to the concept of the awards ceremony. In 2008, they won The Meteors 'Best International Album' award and JUNO 'Alternative Album of the Year' award for their second album, *Neon Bible*, in addition to previous Grammy nominations in the same year for *Neon Bible* and in 2005 for *Funeral*. However, their subsequent appearances did not previously spark such bizarre and unwarranted objections. No one seems to know why.

13

If this was merely a story of a gang of young musicians evolving from a singular obsession with the music of Manchester and post-punk Britain, then the heart of Arcade Fire would seem achingly familiar. In fact, it is nothing of the sort, and in the softer echoes of the mainstream-friendly *The Suburbs*, it is something immediately identifiable, immediately uplifting, a rarity in this world of closed genre and, almost, universal lack of fresh musical ambition.

Arcade Fire do not create a sound that slots into any recognisable genre. It is a sound with roots that creep deeply into the past, long before anything with a slightly folksy, bluesy, country edge was referred to as 'Americana'. It reaches back to a land of disparate complexity, where music forms would evolve and roll and mix and gather pace without push of media or hype or expectation.

So let us travel back to the cultural and racial melting pot of North America in the early 1900s, a time and place of harsh rural realities and comparative lawlessness, and where rampant and accepted racism was firmly entrenched into the underside of the Constitution.

Chapter 1

The Al Rey Connection

It is difficult to pinpoint the moment, the year or even the decade where the Arcade Fire story might have began. There are several points of entry. The moment, perhaps, when Win Butler met his future wife, jazz singer Régine Chassagne, at a Montreal art gallery? It could have been the moment he arrived in that bohemian city or, indeed, the final settling of personnel after various false starts.

But in truth, it is a story with powerful roots that run deep into American culture in the first quarter of the 20th century. This is not merely avenues of influence, either, although the fascinating myriad genres of unfolding Americana – folk, blues, swing, jazz, rock, Irish Appalachian and all the complexities therein – are built solidly into the basic bombastic 'sound' of the band. One could happily theorise for 30 pages in regard to roots and source. Mercifully, that's not necessary, for one man's story holds the key.

Alvino McBurney was born in Oakland, California in 1908 but his upbringing in the Bay Area of America's West Coast was truncated at the age of eight when his family upped sticks to start a new life in Cleveland, Ohio. From an early age – before the move, even – Alvino had shown signs of exceptional innovative aptitude. His natural musicianly stirrings were born from obsessive tinkering with several cheap banjos he kept in his bedroom and before long he started to tap into music forms that would normally seem well off the radar of the average eight year old. Something mysterious was certainly happening to this precocious and intriguing young boy. From the earliest of ages, it became apparent that his natural talents were split equally between the aesthetic and the practical, for his desire to tinker away matched his musical experimentation.

Perhaps even more intriguing, at the point of the family's move he had already managed to build himself a radio set. Indeed, just two years later he achieved exalted status as one of the pioneer – and surely youngest – ham operators in the country and, for that matter, the world.

Radio involvement certainly accelerated his thirst for music, the device leading him to early blues recordings of Eddie Lang and Roy Smeck. Energised by this distant exposure, and gifted his first banjo at the age of 10, Alvino taught himself the rudiments before graduating naturally to guitar by the age of 12.

Typical of his nose for invention, it took just three years for the precocious musician to create a device that could be seen as a precursor of the powerful music age to come. Unfortunately, his self-built electric amplifier would not be patented although, deeper into his career, his pioneering work on improved models would gain several succeeding patents, cementing him firmly in place in the pantheon of electric guitar innovation.

He was just 16 when he turned full-time musician, supplying banjo for Cleveland-born, later New York-based band leader Eve Jones. Further energised by the spirit and eclectic possibilities of the city, he spent two years supplying guitar for Phil Spitalny's 'Spitalny Orchestra' before shifting his base to San Francisco to join Horace Heidt and his Musical Heights. During this spell he also managed to work alongside his childhood hero Roy Smeck and, by this time had changed his surname to Rey, presumably as a nod to the Latino craze that was sweeping America at the time.

It was during his spell with Heidt that Rey started to work on the development of a steel guitar and he has since been regarded as a true pioneer of an instrument that would feature heavily in country and blues music. There would be instant recognition for this work, too, as Heidt's band featured heavily on influential national radio stations of the time, with Rey's extraordinary work seemingly at the cutting edge.

By 1935, nationally famous and already hugely influential, Rey found himself hired by the Gibson Guitar Corporation. Arguably the most prestigious and influential company in electric guitar history, it had been alerted to Rey's talents by discovering the old electric 'pick-up' he had fashioned for one of his series on banjos. Excited by the possibilities and eager to find out just how far this innovatory flair could go, the company asked him to work with Chicago-based engineers Lyon and Healy. The resultant pick-up would become recognised as a giant leap forward for evolution of the electric guitar and would be used on the groundbreaking Gibson ES-150, the prototype of which can be found in The Hendrix Museum, in Seattle. He also worked on the development of a guitar 'talk-box' – used by his wife, Louise, standing behind a curtain, singing along to guitar lines created on stage. Many regard this as the true prototype to a widely used rock'n'roll device which found prominence in the mid-seventies, most famously with Peter Frampton.

Tired of working for band leaders (and pioneering electric guitar companies) Rey formed his own band in 1940 and they worked as the Mutual Broadcasting house band for three years, bringing a raft of influential artists to the forefront of American radio. Among these were Zoot Sims, Billy May, Ray Conniff – all big names of the era – before famously filling in for Dinah Shore at New York's Paramount Theatre.

By the early forties, now internationally famous, Rey enjoyed a run of Top 10 hits and Hollywood fame. Only a messy squabble with the Musicians Union and a resultant ban prevented further success at this point. Strangely, the band, including Rey, was obliged to work at the Lockheed Aircraft Factory in Burbank until Rey joined the US Navy for the duration of World War Two.

It is a measure of Rey's esteem that his post-war orchestra secured an immediate contract with Capital Records, scoring a huge hit with a cover of Slim Gaillard's 'Cement Mixer'. The remainder of the forties saw him working in LA.

His later successes included time as musical director for The King

Sisters, which resulted in a hot television series for ABC, and working as the leader of the band at Disneyland in Orange County.

A Mormon, Rey was received into The Church of Latter Day Saints in 1969. He and his wife, Luisa, moved to Salt Lake City, the home of the Mormon Church, in the nineties but even in semi-retirement he continued to perform with a jazz quintet and never lost his thirst for innovation, running a memoir website for his wife and, at home, endlessly 'fiddling' about with electronics. Their daughter, Liza Butler, is the mother of Edwin (Win) Farnham Butler III and William Butler, both later to become members of Arcade Fire.

In 1978, Rey was inducted into the Steel Guitar Hall of Fame in St Louis as "the father of the pedal steel guitar", and continued to accept work for another 15 or so years, though at a reduced pace. "Well, we do touring and I do concerts," he said. "I'm a guest with symphonies, I do a pop concert. We've done quite a few boat tours and I do conventions. And I do some jazz concerts; I like to do that, that's fun."

For example, he joined The King Sisters on a long tour booked by Columbia Artists Festivals, Big Band Cavalcade '85, which stopped in Cuyahoga Falls, Ohio, where he performed a variety of selections, including big band favourites, a medley of Spanish songs ("We call it our Spanish omelette," he joked on stage), and the *William Tell Overture*. A few years earlier, in 1981, he had also displayed his versatility, along with singers Johnny Desmond and Connie Haines, on a similar tour, The Big Band Show, which came to my hometown, Alliance, Ohio.

The familial link with Arcade Fire was neatly sealed in March 2005 when the band recorded a version of Alvino Rey's 'My Buddy' to be released on the 'Neighbourhood (Tunnels)' single.

Chapter 2

Making Plans For Edwin And William

Alvino Rey's grandson – Edwin Farnham Butler III – was born into the Mormon tradition, in the community of Truckee, California, on April 14, 1980, and his brother, William Pierce Butler, was born two years later, on October 6, 1982. In 1984 the family relocated to the 'planned' conservative community at The Woodlands in south-east Texas where the brothers' grew up and shared an interest in the dark secrets that lay behind the outwardly mundane life of the neighbourhood.

The American middle-class of the mid-fifties shared dreams of picket fences and perfect wives, of happy children pedalling their bicycles through leafy lanes, of besuited husbands returning from work each evening, of family trips to lakes at weekends, of car washing and vacuum cleaners. Behind all this was the stock cliché of repressed emotions that would surface so profoundly in American literature and cinema, from John Cheever and Raymond Carver to *Stepford Wives* and *Revolutionary Road*, wherein the apparent sheen of dull respectability masked repressed passion and flaming desire. Well, that's the theory. It could, of course, be the relationship between a perfect, softly lit, middle-class lifestyle and active young minds that tended towards the mildly paranoiac.

Edwin and William slipped gently into Woodlands and, by all accounts, enjoyed a childhood that reflected this gentle but anaemic dream, their lives lovingly mapped out for them, even if the Masonic under-swell of such communities was never too far afield.

The musicianship within the Butler household really came together during Christmas parties when the base instrument, the mother's harp, would provide the basic soundtrack for an evening of carol singing along with all sorts of musical accompaniment. There was a tenuous family link to modern day carols as a member of Artemo Rey's band, Alfred Burt, had written a number of them, 'Silver Bells' arguably becoming the most famous though others had become firm favourites of the Rat Pack Christmas endeavors and, as such, integral to middle-class America. For many Christmases, Alfred would send the Butlers a recording of a self-penned carol, knowing full well that the family would immediately learn to play it and perform it as part of their Yuletide ritual.

One could perhaps read too much into the fact that The Woodlands is a 'master-planned' community – an architect's view of a commuter-belt idyll, modern, bland and, some might say, heartless. Woodlands is situated just 28 miles to the north of Houston to which streams of commuters shunt grimly along Interstate 45, and then grimly back in the evenings, before splintering into the estates that, although mainly lying within the jurisdiction of Houston, also protrude into neighbouring Shenandoah and Conroe, names that still strike a note of fond recognition to anyone whose childhood encapsulated the age of the TV cowboy.

Win and Will Butler's twin Woodlands childhoods might be seen as perfect grounding for lives led in successful if uniformed obscurity. Indeed, the very concept of this suburban idyll seems designed to repress the bohemian instincts that both inherited from their mother and grandfather. However, the area is not without built-in cultural and sporting outlets. Concert venues presenting live classical and rock music featured heavily in the local media and, indeed, the Cynthia Woods Mitchell Pavilion was the home of the Houston Symphony Orchestra while big rock acts like Aerosmith and Alice Cooper were among the many groups to perform there.

Meanwhile, music filled the Butler household, the family stereogram constantly blasting out the repertoire of Grieg, Mozart, Beethoven and Brahms. The boys' mother, Liza, was a harpist, pianist and vocalist of distinction, whose playing echoed around the house throughout the day, its gentility adding to the boys' understanding of musical ambience. It wasn't a completely classical household, however. The parents owned a copy of every Beatles album and at her piano Liza perfected the lighter end of their spectrum, the McCartney ballads like 'The Long And Winding Road' and 'Let It Be'. Both boys would later admit to being 'profoundly affected' by this tasteful blend of classical and classic contemporary. It is not, after all, a bad place to start. It probably goes without saying that while the harp remained largely unplucked by the boys, the piano's steely omnipresence offered an opportunity to tinker playfully away. As such, the natural musical stream continued to flow down the generations: before they had reached their teens, both boys could instantly copy and hold pretty much any tune they heard.

Win Butler would later admit to an unlikely 13-year-old fascination with Def Leppard – though his future wife, Régine Chassagne, would be horrified at the thought. The album in question was their career-defining *Hysteria*. A close friend of the young Win's played 'Pour Some Sugar On Me' from that album constantly and the song certainly had an impact. While out driving with his grandpa one day, Win noticed a Def Leppard cassette on sale in a truck-stop garage. He convinced his mum to buy if for him, only to discover later that it wasn't *Hysteria* at all, but an early Def Leppard album that left him totally cold.

"It was actually horrible, horrible music," he said. "Some of the most horrible over-produced stuff I have ever heard and a real eye-opener. Probably a good thing that I heard it as it drove me completely away from that kind of radio-friendly heavy rock. It gave me a warning sign."

At first Win tossed the cassette aside, vowing never again to listen to friends with less developed musical taste than his own, but then he changed his mind, picked it up and started to listen. There, perhaps, began Will's rockier musical journey.

Naturally, both boys were fully attuned to rock on American radio, though several big acts were anathema to them. Neither, for example, could ever stand to listen to Don McLean's 'American Pie', which they found objectionable in both imagery and phrasing. Equally offensive to their ears, and somewhat more surprising, was a shared dislike of Led Zeppelin, at the time essential listening for any American teen keen to delve into the history of rock music.

"It's odd, that," Will later admitted. "While we were both surrounded by music, there are a lot of classic rock albums that we simply never heard even though our friends played them all the time. An example, perhaps, would be Pink Floyd and *The Wall*, which was something that we just would never listen to. In fact, we never really have. As for Led Zeppelin... you know, I just don't know them that well. Win perhaps more than me. I have no idea why this is because I was always a rock fan. Maybe I will, one day. Maybe it is my missing link."

Win also developed a fondness for more off-the-wall acts from the seventies. A love of Jonathan Richman can be sourced to the first time he heard 'Roadrunner'. He loved the way the seemingly mundane act of driving a car could be transformed into something magical by the simple power of the lyric. 'Cars' and 'driving' would later feature heavily, albeit metaphorically, in his own songwriting. Will became positively fixated with X Ray Spex' underrated saxophonist Laura Logic – she of the erotic cap-at-jaunty-angle – whom he believed was one of the great 'lost artists of punk'. He even kept track of her later – and largely unknown – solo work.

Win and Will's memories of suburbia also include regular trips down Market Street, a string of shops aimed at re-creating the American ideal of 'Main Street' shopping. This was only partly successful because of the nearby, and more modern, Woodland Mall which, by comparison, must have seemed like 'crystal rooms' to the boys, a palace filled with doughnuts, jellybeans and all manner of retail distractions.

More exciting still, it bordered a large waterway which offered the brothers the thrill of the 'Waterside taxis' and pleasant meandering paths. This central retail core was supplemented by a series of outlying villages, where less-corporate businesses vied for the family shop. Once it had become firmly established as this sort of community, things started to happen to the area, expanding the original planning concept towards environmental principles way ahead of their time and not strictly in tune with the vaguely sinister notion of a place where lives were lived out in a somewhat rigid fashion. This concept of design with nature in a living, breathing community was based on ideas of visionary author and architect Ian McHarg.

It might also be noted that the Butler family arrived in the wake of Hurricane Alicia which, in 1983, wiped away many of the thousands of trees that had been planted in accordance with the design-with-nature concept.

Edwin was a tinkerer, be it with radio, hi-fi or messing with musical instruments. Both practical and aesthetic, he had inherited from his grandfather a thirst for invention as well as musical aptitude and a profound sense of musicality. He also inherited a work ethic that would place him firmly at the helm of his future band. By night, Edwin spent long hours attempting to copy music from his radio. He also seems to have developed a romantic view of radio, which harked back to the days of the sixties, fumbling with wireless knobs in the darkness, hoping to pick up specialist radio stations. As he stated to *Pitchfork*: "I had heard about the pirate stations in Britain in the sixties and always felt that I would love to have experienced that feeling that you are listening to something illicit. Unfortunately I had pretty much every form of music on tap. I was spoilt. Probably a really good thing but I do like the idea of the romance of old radio rather than all music being available at all times. That takes away some of the magic, though I guess it gets music instantly to areas around the world."

With Edwin, was it nature or nurture? Those old rivals certainly began to kick firmly against each other as his musicality developed. He was born with the gift of 'instant read' – the ability to pick out a tune after one hearing rather than having to study the sheet music for a week before attempting to play it. Clearly, there must have been a second-generation handing over of some kind of baton, be it in muse or practical form, but Edwin Farnham Butler was always his own man, often lost in his own world, be it in the darkness of his bedroom or wandering aloof through the streets. He was also the son of an oilman and a harp- and piano-playing mother who loved to sing; contrasting influences of classical and romantic, practical and aesthetic, graft and academia, all bound up in a young man with ambition.

The famous prep school that Win attended – The Phillips Exeter Academy – lies 50 miles north of Boston and was established at the dawn of American democracy, in 1781. Future pupils would include the sons of two Presidents, Lincoln and Grant, as well as a plethora of great American novelists including the mighty Gore Vidal, the bombastic Peter Benchley and the best-selling Dan Brown, author of *The Da Vinci Code*, the merits of which would be hotly debated. Perhaps it is no surprise, therefore, that the school is blessed with the 'largest library of any secondary school in the world'.

Win was a mere 15 when his Phillips Exeter schooling began. It was a wrench, to say the last, from the leafy softness of Woodlands, and his allotted dorm, Abbot Hall, brought with it a not entirely warming legacy. It was daunting, bulging with noisy ghosts, distant echoes and constant reminders of a dark past, full of harrowing tales of doom-laden historic rituals; each one an eerie reminder of a dark past, far darker than mere bullying and braggadocio. The dorm was founded by John Abbot, a semi-famous 18th-century scholar whose infamous links to the occult seeped into the very fabric of Abbot Hall life, if not into the very walls. The dark secrets rippled down through the generations, no doubt gaining in intensity, certainly twisting to suit the contemporary and settling within a complex and ritualistic hall hierarchy that would tightly bind many 'Abboters' long after they had left and entered industry, banking or politics.*

Because of the dorm's physical position – at the very centre of the campus – it would naturally be regarded as the central manifestation of the Academy ethos and, indeed, its mystical undercurrent. Not every graduating 'Abboter' would remain fogged by such rituals although it is difficult to imagine how any aspiring and sensitive artist could fail to find the muse stirred by such historic mystique.

If the musical tastes of the Butler brothers were far from identical, there was one inspirational genre that seemed to unite them, and unites them still. They were – and remain – avid readers of sci-fi books, often citing Philip K. Dick as a key influence, something they share with

---

* In 1996, a fire that ripped through the lower floors was actually blamed on a quickly aborted attempt to contact the hall's founder through a particularly complex and sinister fire ritual.

many British post-punk bands, most famously The Fall, Magazine and The Pop Group. Dick's prolificacy and understanding of the paperback medium meant that he became almost a required read for bands of that generation, his unique contemporary vision seeming to melt well into the background of music and lyrics.

The brothers both share the same favourite novel, albeit not a well-thumbed Dick tome but *Ender's Game* by Orson Scott Card, a futuristic tale set on Earth that presents a view of an exhausted mankind, reeling after surviving two wars with an insect-infested alien world*. In preparation for a third conflict, the Earth leaders enrol children into a 'fight school' to learn the arts of war. It is an oddly compelling read, curiously adopted as required reading for many military organisations, including the US Marines. This link between the present and a fictional future is something that particularly appealed to the brothers.

Significantly, the Butler brothers also claim a love of J G Ballard and it is not difficult to see evidence of this within their work, in particular, in *The Suburbs*. Both Arcade Fire and Ballard seem fond of lyrical references to vast emptiness, suffocating boredom and a mysterious evil undertone to everyday activity. There is even a Ballard quote that appears to cement this link: "Everything has happened... the future is just going to be a vast, conforming suburb of the soul." Quetioned about this, Win suggested that, despite images of mass boredom, there would always be interesting and nutty people who will make life well worth writing about.

Despite the macabre distractions of life in Abbot Hall, Win Butler flourished on all levels at Phillips Exeter. Given his unusual height, he had a natural aptitude for varsity basketball and softball and – given the American penchant for sporting prowess – this enhanced rather than hindered his general schooling. In addition he joined extra-curriculum music clubs that launched him on a voyage of discovery with like-minded students. This spawned a number of embryonic bands, among them the latterly infamous and appallingly named Willy Wonka & The

---

* Building on the critical success of the book, Card wrote several subsequent novels in the series.

Chocolate Factories whose raw, brash sub-thrash suggested more than a touch of irony in their choice of name.

By all accounts Win did more than merely float through early studenthood, his thirst for a sense of involvement drawing him into the students union where he promoted a belief that hard-working students deserved a break during the savage, bitingly cold New England winters. Having written several essays on the importance of countering the extreme weather conditions and attended endless meetings with the college principles, Win managed to establish a concept called 'Winter Thaw', a flexible holiday break that could stretch across a long weekend and which often turned into one great long party. Win would often book, provide and perform musical accompaniment to 'Winter Thaw' events, a concept now firmly established which adds to the eccentricity of the college.

It is well-known that Win Butler's thirst for musical exploration became established while dabbling with the assorted bands at the Phillips Exeter Academy. He has spoken often about his attraction to the all-consuming allure of English alternative and indie. "The music that had been coming out of England for 20 years or so had a profound effect on me," he said. "I was a typical student, in many ways, but perhaps not so drawn towards American metal or grunge... and none of the hair metal appealed at all. But I would spend entire evenings in my dorm with a Cure album, say, or a lot of post-punk stuff, which really fascinated me. It seemed such an explosion of creativity rather than musicianship... that's what really appealed."

He was particularly drawn to the bands of Manchester: Joy Division, New Order, James and The Smiths. "Those bands meant, and still mean, everything to me. They remain built deeply into my musical approach... and it's the same with the rest of the band. New Order... wow, man, I just listened and listened and, of course, The Smiths. Morrissey is quintessentially English and, naturally, that is fascinating to someone like me. I didn't get many of the references in Morrissey's lyrics... I didn't know the films or places, especially in Manchester, but he created a world from his everyday existence. That is what an artist does. That is what I knew I would do... one day. Well, it planted a seed."

Win is fond of recalling the moment when, back in Junior High, he began to understand the difference between Nirvana – the real deal, perhaps – and Bush, who could be said to be somewhat contrived. "That was a big moment. It was the moment that things clicked into place. I then found I could travel back through music and pick up albums by, say, Echo & The Bunnymem, The Cure and The Smiths. I had started to understand what was real and what wasn't. It was something of an eye opener. And these bands took me places… magical places that were partly from the imagination. I started to believe that I might be able to do the same… with Montreal… with my own past experience, however dull it may have seemed."

The 'seed' might seem obvious, in retrospect. Morrissey's Manchester was created from the experience of existing beneath the leaden skies of Stretford, dreaming about The New York Dolls and Oscar Wilde and using those diverse and unconnected influences to colour a life that was hitherto steeped in Mancunian drabness. As such, it might be said that Morrissey's landscape didn't really exist. Manchester provided the template for a lively mind. When Arcade Fire faced the writing of their crucial third album, *The Suburbs*, it saw Butler – among the others – retreating to the mundane life of The Woodlands and expanding from that base, through a darkly surreal dreaming experience that produced a template and a final work drawn from half-remembered happenings, all delicately touched by the nuances of memory.

Win Butler wanted to be a writer. That was his starting point, and remains so, but his desires were multi-media. He yearned to be a photographer, filmmaker or a musician. Or all four.

After graduating with a degree in religious studies – an area that would also connect his past with his oncoming muse – he moved to the Sarah Lawrence College in New York State, a more artistic-based college blessed with a record of outstanding alumni. Previous attendees included film-maker Brian De Palma, journalist Barbara Walters, author Alice Walker, actress Carrie Fisher, jazz vocalist Stacey Kent, singer Carly Simon and photographer Linda Eastman McCartney. Win's intention was to immerse himself in the study of creative writing and photography. The course, however, was flexible and offered the opportunity to combine both disciplines. Win enjoyed his early months, working on a series of projects that would begin with staid photographic images – of trees or random everyday scenes – and then write essays that would expand from those images into imaginative sketches. It wasn't entirely successful and he reacted badly to criticism from tutors who regarded his flamboyant texts as 'just a little too unstructured'. Win felt unhappy to be 'templated' in this way and thundered against the restrictive nature of the courses.

He left the college after a year. He still had his degree to fall back on but, more practically, his needed to slake his thirst for some kind of aesthetic freedom. Relocating to Boston, his intention now was to pull away from academic life and concentrate fully on music. As previously noted, there are many places where the band that would become known as Arcade Fire might begin. Tracing the source is to encounter many roots, stretching back to the muse of Alvino Rey, life in the suburbs, fleeting time in Boston or the eventual meeting of Win Butler and his future wife, Régine Chassagne.

But, perhaps one has to concede that it lies within the restless muse and drive of Win Butler, back in Boston at the dawn of the millennium.

In true indie band tradition, the branches took root within the dorms and corridors at New Hampshire, when Win's musical ambition was being fired by night sessions spent drinking beer and listening to records by The Smiths and New Order with various classmates.

Nevertheless, he returned constantly to the first record he ever purchased, The Cure's singles collection, *Staring At The Sea*. He was astonished to realise the power and possibility of songs with the immediacy of pop yet which seemed to darken with each listen – songs built around dramatic and sexy emotions that were presented in such a light form. Why were The Cure, in particular, different than most other bands, especially in America, where genre categorisation was considered the norm? The Cure, however, achieved their aims on two levels. Their biggest singles – 'The Love Cats', 'Inbetween Days', 'Friday I'm In Love' – were irresistibly hooky and could be enjoyed purely for their effervescence. But even 'The Love Cats', which could have appealed to any eight year old, offers glimpses of something more darkly alluring.

Of course, Butler was soon tempted to explore further and found that there are, in effect, two parallel 'Cures'. As The Manic Street Preachers would go on to do later, The Cure created albums that wavered between jaunty and difficult. They were and remain a band that flies between the light and the dark.

"The idea of using what is technically pop music to convey a heavy emotion always appealed to me," he emailed this writer in 2010. "It was through people like The Cure that immense possibilities seemed to open up. It astonished me that it was still possible, despite the tendency for radio playlists to remain completely safe, dull and unthreatening... that is was still possible for people to break through that and express things that would be beyond the understanding of radio playlists and yet [be] easily absorbed by the fans on the other side."

This fascinating quote indicates that Win Butler was already beginning to understand that, despite opinions to the contrary, is was still possible to get something unique, something truly idiosyncratic, through the system. He dreamed of a mainstream band that still had something important to say. It was a revelation that fired his imagination. This, indeed, might be the moment that Arcade Fire began.

Back in the dormitory came the first true stirrings. Sitting cross-legged in front of his bed, Win would strum chords, scribble words... try more chords, expand slightly, before playing through his unpolished, clunky ideas. While various classmates joined him on occasion, Win's aspirations moved forward considerably when his songwriting sessions attracted classmate Josh Deu. For once the sessions became two-way affairs, with Deu not only sharing Butler's love of – mainly – English indie rock but weighing in with ideas of his own. As the year 2000 progressed, songs started to take shape, slowly at first and then, according to Win, "A torrent of ideas flowed between us which surprised even me."

Encouraged by the progress of their songwriting sessions, Butler and Deu made plans to record a tentative demo. As 2001 dawned, Win found himself torn between the idea of launching some kind of band in Boston or relocating to Canada where Deu felt opportunities were more plentiful. This latter course would take Win to the heart of the Montreal scene during the summer, by which time he would be armed with a demo recorded with Deu, neatly augmented by multi-instrumentalist Brendan Reed – who was also able to supply some of the vocals – and various local musicians including Tim Kyle, Myles Broscoe and Dane Mills.

The demo sessions would eventually surface in bootleg form much to Butler's distress, though there is no credible reason why. They contain none of the musical naiveté one might expect from a first foray into a recording studio. Indeed, if anything, the songs sound startlingly mature, more so perhaps than the songs that would later surface on the official Arcade Fire demos, which betrayed plenty of feverish juvenile hysteria. These earlier recordings offer a strangely 'settled' musicality in songs that suggest a distant pre-echo of the 'softened' approach the band would eventually adopt for their all-encompassing third album, *The Suburbs*.

'In The Attic' – a song that might be said to contain lyrical hints of Tom Waits – was embellished by mandolin and woodwind accompaniment, reminiscent of R.E.M. circa *Automatic For the People*, just before the Athens favourites junked their cult credentials and hurtled into a more radio friendly and hugely successful approach.

'Accidents' is similar in feel, though it carries a wry tone that again could eventually be glimpsed during the lighter moments on *The Suburbs*.

'Winter For A Year' might be said to be a meditation on the Boston weather, but it also contains the kind of Narnian atmosphere of Arcade Fire's 'Neighbourhood' song sequence at the heart of their first album, *Funeral*.

But these first three songs are overshadowed by the grand sweeping musical statement on the auspicious 'The Great Arcade Fire'. Not only is this song the genuine source of the band's eventual moniker, it was also a reflection of the surreal nature of a childhood spent in the suburbs. Already we see Win Butler dipping into evocations of his own past and pulling something remarkable out of the depths of ordinariness. That young boy, wheeling around the driveways of Woodlands on his bicycle, lost in a dream state amid the clipped lawns and carefully tended gardens, was unwittingly storing memories for the future. The line "The Christmas tree is on fire" leaps from the song and is born from nothing more than the imagination of a little boy contemplating the family Christmas tree and the myriad colours thrown by the lights. More than that, however, is the brooding intensity of the backing on 'The Great Arcade Fire' which would be used to such staggering effect to create the overpowering atmosphere on *Funeral*.

So where did the notion of an 'Arcade Fire' come from? Often, in the future, Win would brush the question away, softly stating: "A friend of mine told me a story of this fire at a local arcade. I don't know whether the story was true or not and I never looked into it. But the phrase stuck in my mind."

While this deflection is certainly believable – Win perhaps just going with his instinct – the story impressed him enough to inspire him to write an evocative song about it, perhaps of some imaginary and, yes, 'great' arcade fire. In the UK the word arcade immediately conjures up visions of some faded fifties seaside summer palace, full of whirring slot machines and pastel colours – with the 'fire' effectively destroying that decaying ambience forever – in the US it is more likely to be a shopping arcade, still an ageing concept in the days before gigantic shopping malls, a place with quaint independent shops and a non-corporate atmosphere. In this way the phrase Arcade Fire might even hint at the demise of the individual in the face of the corporate bully. Either way, the title suggests a yearning for something that has died, be it physical or, more pertinently, musical. A band called Arcade Fire would surely carry some sense of history within their music as, of course, would be the case. That stated, when I first mentioned the name of this band back in 2005 to unimpressed friends, they naturally assumed it to be the name of some new thrash metal band. Names, of course, alter with increasing familiarity and become less relevant.

Win moved to Montreal soon after the demo recordings. Though initially Deu's idea, Win was only too happy to follow suit and seek out a fresh scene in which to progress musically. It seemed like the right move even though he initially regarded Montreal as "the coldest place on Earth".

Why Montreal? For Win Butler, who had wavered for a few months before finally taking the plunge, the city represented the nearest place that would allow him to tap into a local music scene large enough to have international implications. The city may not have anything remotely on the scale of New York's cultural melting pot, or LA's rock cool or even Chicago's blues heritage but it did have a legacy of its own. In terms of Canada, it is generally regarded as the 'Cultural Capital of the Country', at least according to Canada's *Monocle* magazine which has a talent for spotting such things.

From the city's bohemian heart, a thriving media industry has developed alongside the many cultural communities in a city that is the centre for French language television programmes, radio, theatre, film, digital and print media. It has an enviable tradition in pop, rock and jazz, with a number of independent labels operating from downtown, bolstered by a heavy summer season of arts festivals which serve to bring the varying communities together. Particularly famous – and, indeed, important to the formation of Arcade Fire – is the Montreal International Jazz Festival, which attracted the attentions of a young, jazz-soaked Haitian called Régine Chassagne, the Montreal World Film Festival and the French-based Nuits d'Afrique.

As Win immediately discovered, the Place des Arts (Eastern downtown) offers a configuration of concert halls supporting one of the world's greatest orchestras, the Montreal Symphony Orchestra, whose strains and refrains hang in the air on any given Saturday evening, and acts as a backdrop for many avant garde dance troupes and street performers. Put all this together and add the hugely evocative architectural heart – many buildings of historical importance in the old town, including Notre-Dame de Montreal Basilica and the powerful presence of all the major Canadian banks, on St James Street – and you can imagine a young Win Butler wandering through the city centre, with the buildings, the music swirling in the air, the frenetic bohemian pace, setting his imagination soaring. What a perfect place to discover a penchant for baroque rock music. What a perfect place to create a sound practically carved from the city centre atmosphere. Win was always fond of the notion that 'architecture is frozen music' and the reverse process, prizing music from the inspiration of buildings, could well produce the kind of distinctive sound he was searching for.

In addition, the city is small enough to retain the kind of village atmosphere capable of supporting a vibrant music scene, small enough, perhaps, for an out of town lad to start to make his mark both locally and internationally.

This, at least, was the theory. However the fact that Arcade Fore would rise from this city scene owed less to any sense of 'scene' and much more to the sheer bloody-minded attitude of a musician and then a set of musicians determined to climb from the city's bohemian heart without actively belonging to it.

Nevertheless, few would argue against the notion that this lovely, evocative city would strongly flavour the oncoming surge of music of Arcade Fire.

What's more, once there, things happened quickly.

"I felt like I discovered Montreal," Win told Paul Morley in *The Observer*.

"Obviously I didn't, but I came and went, holy shit, I never even looked at this place on the fucking map, and there's this great weird city, and it's full of arts and culture, and I was so shocked. A year in Boston, nothing. I come to Montreal, and I had a performing band straight away. It's hard not to think of it as fate that I found myself there."

In terms of music, Montreal has a uniquely diverse place in Canada's history. It has been universally noted for having unlikely krautrock, synthesiser and electronic connections, partly because of the success of Men Without Hats in the eighties ('Safety Dance'), although they were to re-emerge in the nineties in a guitar-driven form, and partly because of the kind of clubs that peppered the city centre, attracting a New Romantic ethos and a plethora of bands that sprung up to support it.

It is no surprise to discover that German electronic pioneers Kraftwerk were particularly big in Montreal, and local Madonna-esque pop tart Mitsou became a clubland regular with her dance hit 'Bye Bye Mon Cowboy'.

The electronic tag aside, Montreal's music truly spans a wide range of genres, with examples of punk, metal, pop and rock. Indeed, one of the significant elements of the city is that both in terms of local festivals and in the clubs, many concerts feature acts from all these genres on the same bill. While electronic may have been the guiding light, it is rare to find fans of such disparate music forms mixing freely with no hint of rivalry; in short, it's a city of musical acceptance. In terms of Arcade Fire, this is immensely significant. While their electronic angle may be difficult to locate, it does suggest that their diverse and unusual instrumentation was more likely to find acceptance in Montreal than many other places.

Folk music was another genre that found a welcome in the city and this also had a profound effect on Win Butler. The folk boom of the sixties may have faded elsewhere but in Montreal it carried into the eighties, famously so within Canadian circles. This so-called late folk music soon merged – unlikely as it might sound to British eras – with the electronic heart of clubland. Men Without Hats became the only act from this genre to gain international recognition, but beyond them could be found Heaven Seventeen (not the Sheffield post-punkers, but another band who took the name from the band in *A Clockwork Orange*), Rational Youth, The Box and Isinglass.

There are many reasons for this. Several artists and musicians chose to move to Montreal simply because it is relatively cheap to live there. Unlike, say, central Toronto, it is even possible to get by working in bars and running a band simultaneously. Cheap rents in student-like abodes were often the norm and contributed significantly to the city's bohemian edge.

At first, though, Win Butler was slightly lost and aloof in this cold, cold town. Despite a continuing friendship with Deu, he felt like a true outsider, hanging around the fringes of gigs, listening to the tales of burgeoning local bands, attempting to make friends, urging involvement. In an effort both to kick-start his floundering musical ambitions and as a way of meeting people, he started to bring musicians together.

The ersatz band would spend the latter half of 2001 and early 2002 edging into local performances, often at loft parties, art galleries, sparsely attended college halls and cafes. Mostly the gigs would be procured via friends of the band. No one, in effect, knew how to gain the attentions of local agents or journalists.

"I was embarrassed," admitted Win in 2011. "I was simply exploding with ambition and yet didn't really have a clue. It never dawned on me to contact local newspapers and try and get a bit of a name. We just plugged away, getting nowhere, really."

This apparent inertia proved too frustrating for Myles Broscoe, whose relationship with Win Butler had started to show considerable strain, both in rehearsal and in performance, although not to electrifying effect. A modest musical spat became more personal as both attempted to wrestle control of the band's songwriting process. Almost immediately Broscoe was replaced by Richard Reed Parry. In the background, and soon to emerge as another potent element of the band to be known as Arcade Fire, was the less noticeably flamboyant figure of Will Butler, Win's younger brother.

William Butler graduated from Phillips Exeter Academy in 2001. Unlike Win, he showed no interest in the study of religion but his time alone in the dorm did give him a chance to build a musical base, although he wasn't so dismissive of American rock and enjoyed the work of, among many others, Dinosaur Jr and Nirvana.

After graduation, he moved to Northwestern University in Chicago where, following his individual muse, he read poetry and Slavic studies. Indeed, poetry was his first love at the time and he soon progressed to the position of editor at the university's acclaimed poetry organ, *Helicon*. This lively magazine gained a readership far beyond the confines of the campus and an excerpt from a poem included in his thesis is quoted in a book by Brian Bouldrey, *Honorable Bandit: A Walk Across Corsica.**

While at Northwestern, Will's artistic activity wasn't confined to poetry. His love of mainline American rock music led to him finding

---

* Published in September 2007, by Terrace Books, *An Honorable Bandit* sees the author taking a leather-bound journal to the island of Corsica, intent on making a travelogue of a hike across the island. In many ways, *Honorable Bandit* feels like a transcription of that finished journal. It captures the walk across Corsica as if Bouldrey was writing it down minute by minute, speckled with random trail observations and going off into the sort of thoughts one gets when moving your feet is all the challenge you need. However, the journal motif extends far enough to leave the book a touch disjointed. The book follows Bouldrey and his friend Petra on a hike through the diagonal length of the island. As the two head down the path, Bouldrey shares his thoughts on the sweeping or painful mountain ranges, esoteric fellow hikers and the island's unique customs. He's certainly chosen the right area to take a walk: politically French but culturally apart, birthplace of the family vendetta and a history peppered with invasions.

work as a DJ, initially during low-key college events and later with a regular spot for the WNUR Rock Show, broadcasting on 89.3 FM. This is the station of Northwestern University and prides itself on an eclectic musical diversity, with shows featuring streetbeat, reggae, jazz, blues, soul, continental drift and rock. The station, subtitled Chicago's Sound Experiment, is intended to reflect the legacy and continuing openness of Chicago music. Soon he would hire Nathan Amundson, later of Rivulets, as a substitute DJ on the station.

Chapter 3

From Haiti With Love

The next key development in the evolution of Arcade Fire was the arrival of Régine Chassagne, who was born in Montreal on August 18, 1977, and grew up in the gentle suburb of St Lambert, to the south of the city. But Régine's story truly began 15 years earlier when her parents emigrated from their native Haiti to escape the snapping jaws of the François Duvalier dictatorship.

Duvalier, who was in office from 1957 until 1971, first won acclaim in fighting diseases, earning him the nickname 'Papa Doc'. He opposed a military coup d'état in 1950, and was elected President in 1957 on a populist and black nationalist platform. His rule, based on a purged military, a rural militia and the use of a personality cult and voodoo, resulted in the murder of an estimated 30,000 Haitians and an ensuing 'brain drain' from which the country has yet to recover. Ruling as President for Life from 1964 until his death in 1971, Duvalier was succeeded by his son, Jean-Claude, nicknamed, somewhat lazily, 'Baby Doc'.

While his political position in the would could only be defended by the sheer complexity of Haiti's situation, Duvalier's lasting legacy, which still leaves a dark cloud over the country to this day, remains his savage purging of all things vaguely communist, resulting in the deaths of many thousands. Many educated professionals, fearing they would be regarded at "intellectually at odds with Governmental ethos, and therefore a threat and at great risk", would literally flee for their lives. In simplistic terms, the Duvalier regime would rid Haiti not only of political extremists, but of talented, forthright professionals, artists and writers who could have provided a true continuum of the country's rich and varied culture. The country would eventually fight back from the extremes of aesthetic blandness that often follows dictatorial paranoia, but much colour had been lost.

The Haiti story, from 'Papa Doc' to the 2010 earthquake, would feature heavily in the lyrical and musical spread of Arcade Fire, the lost beauty and talent resurfacing most obviously in the song 'Haiti', featuring the line, "Mes cousins jamais nes hantentles nuits de Duvalier" ("My unborn cousins haunt Duvalier's nights").

Chassagne studied communications at Concordia University, graduating with a BA in 1998. During her time at Concordia, she found that her deepest calling was music performance and, utilising her extensive natural musicality, she regularly practised and performed within campus events on accordion, xylophone, drums, hurdy gurdy, keyboards and organ as well as experimenting wildly with alternative percussion.

She admits that this extensive list of instrumental skills brought with it a number of problems, not least the choice of musical style or genre, which are, more often than not, defined by a musician's limitations. Even at student level, it became clear that the band that would contain Régine Chassagne would be most extraordinary, expansive and open to a rich seam of constant musical and thematic ideas. But could such a band even exist, let alone drift through her close-knit college circle? It seemed unlikely.

Well, perhaps not. Chassagne's first encounter with a serious musical unit might seem slightly bizarre, although, given the traditional spread of her music, her period within the ranks of an accomplished Montreal-based medieval band might not seem so strange, especially given the band's instrumentation.

The band in question were Les Jongleurs de la Mandragore. Formed in 1995, they had crafted a powerful critical reputation during their formative years. Indeed, Susie Napper, artistic director of the Montreal Baroque Festival, noted: "Ensemble Mandragore is one of Montreal's most exciting young Early Music groups to emerge in the past five years. Both connoisseurs and the public at large appreciate their amusing, dynamic concerts that stand as the perfect introduction to Medieval music. Highly recommended!"

Mandragore's music has a powerful effect on its listeners, similar to those attributed to the mythical mandrake plant for whom they are named. The ensemble specialises in European music of the 12th to 14th centuries. The Artistic Director of this Early Music ensemble is Ingried Boussaroque (soprano, recorders, crumhorn and harmonium), and François Taillefer (percussion) acts as co-director. The other members include Sean Dagher (cittern and hurdy-gurdy), Tobie Miller (soprano, flutes, recorder and hurdy gurdy) and Andrew Wells-Oberegger (oud, lute, bouzouki).

This medieval music ensemble boasts two distinguishing factors: first, an explosive energy and dynamism, and second, a musical approach that combines both musicological rigour and contemporary creativity. Mandragore adds catchy rhythms, languorous voices, rich chords and unexpected colours to medieval melodies. The results speak for themselves: invitations, concerts, recordings, etc. They have performed all over Quebec at festivals and period events. Mandragore has graced all manner of venues from Quebec City's Musée de la Civilisation to Montreal's Kola Note.

The musicians of the Mandragore love to present rare instruments and share stories behind the music and historical context. Their performances seduce audiences of all ages, from neophytes to connoisseurs, but despite their local success and high degree of musicianship, the limitations of performing medieval music were all too obvious and Chassagne yearned for a greater musical adventure. The lure of jazz, never too far away in Montreal, began to pull and she briefly entered McGill University to study 'jazz voice'.

She also performed some solo gigs that would, in time, become the stuff of legend. Lost to her own percussive sway, she quite literally built up sound from anything, a heating pipe, a drain, biscuit tins or, more traditionally, tambourines. It was the art of simplistic performance, lower than low-fi and, in terms of status, barely rising above the buskers who struggled to attract the attentions of the Montreal commuters. Chassagne was sassy enough to stretch beyond the street, however, performing in semi-comedic manner to works Christmas parties and weddings, literally pulling a rhythm out of thin air, getting that ungainly uncle out of the chair. The girl had rhythm and charm. Drumless but blessed with beat, she had no way of knowing it but she was engaged in the necessary intensive training for her role among the ranks of Arcade Fire. She would become the pulse and the frisson. She would be capable of tugging a song this way or that by slight alterations in tempo and all within the guise of performance, all within the explosive musical personality that she nurtured in the office parties of Montreal,

She also longed for jazz. At 15, the first music she had ever bought had been a cassette collection of songs by Billie Holiday. The introduction to Holiday had a profound effect on her, taking her clean away from mainstream radio to a world beyond, where a different kind of tension lay ready to be explored. She had never before heard such singing and it was certainly unusual for one so young to be drawn to an artist like Holiday. After all, American-based 15-year-old-girls are more naturally led towards pretty but numbingly inane blonde pseudo-country starlets with their own television series than long-dead jazz singers who sang about 'Strange Fruit', Holiday's euphemism for Negroes lynched by southern racists.

Billie Holiday changed Régine's perception of music. Holiday's vocal phrasing offered a new challenge and a fresh way of expression. Using the determination that would continue throughout her career, she spent long hours in her bedroom singing along with Holiday's distinctive tones. "I taught myself to sing jazz. It was like learning another language but, I guess, I did it at an early age so it didn't seem so bad. Nobody around me seemed to be listening to that kind of music but I loved the way that history had been built into it."

Strictly speaking, the vocal phrasing owed as much to the blues although, either way, it was becoming obvious that Régine Chassagne would never completely share the rock sensibilities of the boys who would one day form the larger part of the band she joined. Before that, however, lay further jazz explorations.

Speaking to *Uncut* magazine in July 2011, she said: "I sang and played accordion in a jazz band called Azúcar. I was always into jazz. I remember hearing a Charlie Parker solo on the car radio when I was 13. I recognised the chord sequence and realised what it meant to improvise over a tune. It was like a light switching on in my head. Aha! I understand jazz."

Happy to be lost in jazz, albeit locally, Chassagne performed chanteuse-style vocals, often accompanied by a traditional trio, at the trendier restaurants and art galleries in the city. Indeed, it was at one such event – an art opening at Concordia University – that her vocal talents were observed with enthusiasm by Win Butler, at that point attempting to form a band of his own. Although he had no idea that, behind that extraordinary voice, also lay an unfathomable array of musical aptitude, he was more than charmed by this talented, attractive and petite lady who was brimming with confidence and a charisma unlikely in a singer booked at a wine-sipping, art-musing event.

If there is another moment when the story of Arcade Fire could be said to have began, this is it: this split second when Win Butler glanced towards Régine Chassagne, and something clicked on so many levels. It was a moment when the sharp end of two cultures collided. In time, Régine and Win would fall in love, marry and work closely together as the beating heart of one of the biggest and most culturally intriguing bands on the planet, the romantic side of Arcade Fire, where their passion, adoration and affection would spin continuously, adding flair and spark to the music and to this story.

That day – the first time Win ever had seen her face – was the day that he asked Régine to join his, admittedly failing, Montreal band, a collection of raggedy student-come-musos with one foot in a downbeat, grey rock base and another locked into a series of low-key gigs of little merit and less applause.

Régine has stated that she was attracted to Win's "deep seriousness and open, intense sense of ambition". There is no doubt that, as the two

41

began to talk that evening, something special occurred. Win seemed to be a deeply driven fellow who needed someone with a vast and accomplished musicality to help him realise his ambitions. In retrospect, it is difficult to think of a single other person on earth more perfectly suited to this than Régine Chassagne. Petite, charming, precociously talented and ferociously driven herself, she even had the instrumental prowess to allow Win's songs to unfold to their full potential,

Something tangible did happen that night: a loose suggestion about trying "a few musical things together"' resulted in a song, to all intents and purposes fully written by the end of the evening. The song was called 'Headlights Look Like Diamonds' and it would see the light of day on the debut Arcade Fire EP. It was a song that strongly suggested an all-encompassing and stadium-friendly 'sound' – a sound that was discovered by accident and would represent a freak of nature, not just with the coming together of Win and Régine, but of all the respective components of a band that would be, at once, both complex and simplistic.

Chapter 4

The Tolling Of The Bell

The Bell Orchestre is a six-piece instrumental band from Montreal, which has been providing highly charged gigs in the city since their inception in 2001. As their name suggests, they offer a heady fusion of orchestral music heavily spiced with the spirit of rock. The links with Arcade Fire are therefore obvious on first listen, both from the scope, power and accessibility of their music and the fact that two key members of Bell Orchestre would become full time members of Arcade Fire, while continuing to spend time in the Orchestre's ranks. The links would strengthen further as the two musical units would record their debut albums simultaneously and even tour together in the immediate aftermath.

Among the ranks of the Bell Orchestre is Richard Reed Parry. Born in October, 1977 in Ottawa, Parry earned a local reputation, initially as a double-bassist in the Montreal unit New International Standards, alongside guitarist/bass guitarist Tim Kingsbury, also to be brought into the ranks of Arcade Fire.

Parry's early introduction to music, somewhat bizarrely, came via exposure to the soundtrack of David Lynch's *Twin Peaks* television series. He was particularly entranced by the powerful atmosphere created by music in a supporting role, which possibly steered him towards music production. It certainly guided him towards a more holistic approach to his music and, without doubt, the Bell Orchestre seems to have been the perfect primer for a role in the musical framework of Arcade Fire.

While the rather gothic *Twin Peaks* soundtrack might have shaped his vision, the first record he purchased was C + C's Music Factory's 'Gonna Make You Sweat (Everybody Dance Now)'. More indicative, one imagines, of a juvenile music moment he shared with friends rather than a true indication of musical ambition. However, he also nurtured a growing fondness for Cat Stevens, an artist whose glory days occurred well before Parry's time but whose enduring simplicity has subsequently cut through time and genre.

"Cat Stevens is loved around the world and yet still remains underrated," claimed Parry in *Uncut* magazine. "He is up there with the Paul Simons and Bob Dylans... not in terms of a mass body of work, obviously, but certainly in the way he changed the course of songwriting, adding mystical and beautifully simplistic lyrics. A true original. I learned a huge amount from the simplicity of Cat Stevens. The idea that a simple song can also be lush, dark and powerful. I would spend hours listening to those records, trying to work out how they had been constructed. The best songs are the ones that might seem very simple but a huge amount of work and thought goes into the background."

Like Régine, Win and Will, Parry was raised in a family soaked in music and performance. Indeed his late father, David Parry, had earned local fame as a member of Friends Of Fiddlers Green, a Toronto-based folk band of some repute. Richard's mother, Caroline Balderstone Parry, was also well-known as a bohemian poet and musician. In addition, his sister Evelyn still performs widely as a singer-songwriter and poet.

At Canterbury High School in Ottawa, Parry's natural bent towards arts and performance saw him become a particularly active member of the Literary Arts Programme – a kind of Ottawan footlights review – alongside Martin Gero, later to write 'Atlantis', and Canadian comedian Kurt Smeaton of *The Holmes Show*.

After graduation, Parry followed his vegetarian instincts and worked as a cook at Camp Au Grand Bois, a summer camp at Chelsea, Quebec.

While he dallied with the idea of entering the catering industry, it was the allure of music that took him back into education, this time by studying electro-acoustics and contemporary dance at Concordia University. His musicality was also eclectic and soon he was performing on celesta, keyboards, piano, organ and synthesizers, guitar, accordian and percussion as well as singing and contributing backing vocals to whatever project caught his imagination.

This extraordinary breadth of instrumental prowess would be unique to even the most accomplished of bands, but as the musicians who would make up Arcade Fire fell together in the underside of the Montreal scene, he found himself among similarly gifted bandmates. This unlikely union of scope and musical precocity would soon become part of the general focus of the band, adding precision, determination and a wealth of musical possibilities. Most importantly, this vast array of instrumental diversity added immense depth, not unlike Phil Spector's 'Wall of Sound', and this would become the core element of Arcade Fire – songs of structural simplicity, pumped up into a state of high musical drama.

Parry always regarded himself as a musician, composer and, as stated, producer. It would be this latter role that would seem to be his most comfortable arena; using the wide skyline of musical knowledge (big ears, as they would say), the boy also known as Reedy would eventually become the levelling glue of the Arcade Fire sound.

Alongside Parry in Bell Orchestre – then as now, also in Arcade Fire – is Sarah Neufeld. Born August 27, 1979 on Vancouver Island, British Columbia, Neufeld would become one of the underrated elements of Arcade Fire. Even on stage, she often seems overshadowed by the more obviously upfront Chassagne or, indeed, more bombastic Tim Kingsbury. But Neufeld is a hugely precocious multi-instrumentalist with a musical vision every bit as strong as that of Jeremy Gara or Win Butler. Within the ranks of Bell Orchestre – alongside not just Reed Parry but also Pietro Amatro, one of the fleeting members of the unsteady and embryonic Arcade Fire – she was best known for her thrusting virtuosity on violin. Overshadowed or not, she remains an arresting sight on stage, standing on tiptoe to reach the mic, openly mouthing heartfelt backing vocals while slicing viciously across her instrument, or thumping the keyboards. Effervescent and powerful in performance, she adds a huge sense of sheer joy into the heart of whatever song is being performed. She might be an engine room performer, but when Arcade Fire play without Sarah Neufeld – as has happened on a couple of occasions – an essential element seems noticeably missing; like a hole in the heart.

Neufeld moved from Vancouver to Montreal at the age of 18 alongside electronic artist Tim Hecker and continues to work not just in Arcade Fire and Bell Orchestre but also Montreal band The Luyas.

Tim Kingsbury was a friend and occasional musical collaborator of Parry. Specialising in bass guitar, guitar and keyboards, he spent his formative years living in the vicinity of Guelph, Ontario, where he developed distinctly indie musical leanings, rocking away in the scruffy togs of post grunge to a rack full of albums by Dinosaur Jr, Sonic Youth and The Fall, and bringing a distinctive edge to a number of local bands, The New International Standards, Wolf Parade and Clark The Band among them.

Of these, Wolf Parade became the most successful. They formed in April 2003, when former Frog Eyes member Spencer Krug was offered a gig by Grenadine Records' Alex Megelas. With only a three-week deadline to form a band, Krug contacted fellow Canadian guitarist Dan Boeckner (formerly of British Columbia band Atlas Strategic) and began writing songs in Krug's apartment. In September 2004, they travelled to Portland, Oregon to record with Modest Mouse's Isaac Brock. Brock had recently signed the band to Sub Pop when he was an A&R man for the label at the time.

But Kingsbury's time with Wolf Parade never seemed completely satisfactory. Although a rocker at heart, he wanted to be part of something bigger or some new kind of rock performance, something different from the traditional guitar-bass-drums combo. "I was blown away the first time I saw Arcade Fire," he recalls. "Clean blown away."

Nevertheless, it wasn't a particularly auspicious occasion. "It was Win and Régine and a couple of other people, playing in a loft party in Montreal, and it was really a shambolic mess with equipment that didn't work very well, but there was something magical there."

It was, at once, obviously embryonic and yet it seemed to offer Kingsbury the musical opportunities he craved. "There was a birthing period. Win and Régine were starting to get serious and looking for new people to play with, but I don't think anyone was sure what that meant," he says. "I remember the concept that if you take something beautiful and peaceful and gentle and mash it up with something harsh and aggressive then you might get an interesting combination. Régine was so crazy talented, she could play anything, and Will was able to play different instruments, and it all fell into place. When I started to perform with them, it actually seemed to be a pain in the ass to switch instruments on every song… it really did but, musically speaking, it just seems right."

Kingsbury was starting to tire of the attitudes of many of his grunge heroes. "I was really sick of bands just ignoring the audience as a posture in rock music. And I think we fed off each other in terms of trying to engage the audience, not in a hammy way, but actually trying to be aware of the space that you are playing in, and trying to connect in some way through the music. When we all got together, we kind of brought out that aspect in our personalities, it's like feeding off each other's inhibitions. I think all bands are a work in progress, you kind of figure things out as you go."

Kingsbury is the one member of Arcade Fire who could be genuinely described as a 'Dylanologist', if not the more dedicated 'Bobcat'. Having immersed himself in Dylan's gargantuan body of work throughout his life, he can recite the lyrics of entire albums and, on more than one occasion, has confessed to "nursing a broken heart with a copy of *Blood On The Tracks*". Often defensive of Dylan, he openly distrusts anyone who is dismissive of his Bobness… although one of his best friends, Jeremy Gara, confesses to 'never getting Dylan'.

More surprisingly perhaps, Kingsbury is a self-confessed 'Abba freak' and, should anyone pour scorn on the Swedish group's credibility, will launch into a robust defence, claiming them to be 'almost at Beatles level' in terms of songwriting prowess. He is not alone in this, such disparate characters as Bono, Kurt Cobain and Elvis Costello having all confessed a weakness for Abba. Not surprisingly, Kingsbury is a lover of the all-encompassing Abba sound, their attention to production detail that announces the 'arrival' of any given Abba song within its opening bars. This is significant, as the creation of a full-blown and distinctive 'sound' that can be attributed to an act fascinates Kingsbury, whose input into the eventual and similarly universal sound for Arcade Fire cannot be understated.

Drummer Jeremy Gara was a fellow member of Clark The Band and The New International Standards alongside Tim Kingsbury and it seems almost superfluous to point out that like everyone else involved he is a multi-instrumentalist, also proficient on guitar and keyboards. Born in July 1978 in Ottawa, Gara had already burned his way into the Montreal rock scene by providing significant contributions to the self-titled album by Arizona Amp and Alternator. He'd also played drums briefly with the lesser known (and badly named) rock outfit Weights And Measures, and during his time with the peculiarly bohemian Snailhouse he found himself playing alongside violinist Sarah Neufield.

Chapter 5

Learning Fast

Win Butler, speaking to *Pitchfork*: "Even when we started out playing little art galleries in Montreal, we'd pick up on a certain level of cool stand-offishness in the crowd and just try and break though it. We wanted to connect with the audience in a way that other groups we played with didn't seem to really care about. I guess, in one way, every band ends up doing what they feel other bands should do for them as fans."

Imagine a house party, in Montreal, 2002. There is a downbeat, unusually downcast crowd of people huddled together, mouths agape, dead of eye and curiously vacant. Some are known to others, others not. They were drawn to this house by a promise. A local music collective of some repute would perform while, at the rear of the house, beer and Mohitas would be dished out. Later the partygoers would abandon themselves to typical Saturday night hedonism, random couples pairing off here and there as sexual allure asserts itself, while those excluded from the mating game by virtue of unattractiveness or lifelessness or both conceal their disappointment by mouthing off about politics, arguing arrogantly and bordering on the obnoxious. Tempers might become frayed as the drink takes hold. There might even be the odd fight, although in the end the antagonists would disassemble and eventually collapse into the cold night.

But before that, and before their reluctant eyes, a band would have performed who attempted to cut through the shoe-gazing by performing a song called 'My Heart Is An Apple'. They would summon forth all the guile in their embryonic armoury to achieve this, the curly-haired girl's coy entrancements attempting to pull the crowd's attention into the heart of the music. Mostly she would fail though the attempt is heartening. She attracts a few glances and the rest of the band move somewhat clunkily through the song's curled progression. At one point, in a further attempt to bridge that all too intangible cordon that separates artist from performer, as the girl takes central stage and sings a hearty lead, the tallest member of the group crawls through the crowd's legs. How nervously they shuffle, edging left and right as he snakes among them, almost threatening them with the dreaded call for audience participation. 'My Heart Is An Apple', forms the core of the band's short set. Here they were. Learning fast. Performing before the smallest and most difficult crowds of their career.

Win Butler again: "Performing at Coachella or Glastonbury when well known seems painless when compared to being a young, unknown band, trying like crazy to get some kind of message across to some disinterested house party. I knew, back then, that we would never again have to perform in such a difficult arena. But I also understood how the experience helped shape our onstage attack."

Onstage attack? It was more than that, much more than mere arrogant thrash. It was an attempt at a theatrical projection. At that point, without the gravitas of fame, Arcade Fire had to rely solely on the cold selling of their stagecraft. It was the same at every gig; different faces, same disinterested, vacant stares, same suspicion of any new ensemble, any new bunch of hopefuls and, in Montreal, arguably more than in most cities, a prevailing sense of unease born of conservative taste. It was a place where the term 'local band' carried derogatory meaning until, and in some cases beyond, the thrust of initial success.

For Arcade Fore, a band for whom 'performance' was as important as 'performing', the task seemed even more difficult. Win Butler's spontaneous crawl through the legs of the crowd was seen as openly, appallingly beyond-the-pale behaviour. After all, burgeoning rock acts were supposed to be respectful of their early audiences. How dare they take the performance into the crowd? Who the hell did they think they were?

Just for a moment, as the Arcade Fire sound slowly emerges, it seems important to glance back to the precocious young mind of Alvino Rey and his thirst for invention, his longing for innovation and search for some kind of musical truth amid the always colourful backdrop of 20th-century Americana. Rey's music may have ebbed and flowed with the trends and he was certainly happy to explore new music, whether from Cuba or the Caribbean, Africa or Ireland, but his true legacy was to take those styles of music and blend them into his own, uniquely American take on things. His role as a precursor of Arcade Fire, two generations down, ought not to be understated. This is not simply the handing down of instrumental skills, or even a musical vision, it is far more fundamental than that. Rey's vision was of multi-instrumental collage, a representation, if you like, of North America's unprecedented melting pot; stirred, spiced and served up with the sexual and emotive depth of blues and folk, the wild head-swing of dense jazz (Miles Davis, John Coltrane lurk menacingly in the undertone), the power and force of metal and even, in places, the thrust of punk and grunge.

To achieve such a sound, a sound that changes shape and density, album to album, song to song, it would be necessary to dismantle the traditional dynamics of rock music. Think of a band of multi-instrumentalists, a band of people with differing influences and even goals, a band who change their size and shape with each passing concert, if not each passing song, a band who naturally change instruments, thereby challenging the very process that creates rock music in the first place. This could be achieved, surely, by the kind of band who perform in arts centres in San Francisco, New York and Hartlepool before a bemused gaggle of rag-taggle arts students who sense value and freedom in newly invented techniques. This alone is worth a story, say five pages in the excellent and eccentric *Wire* magazine, perhaps? But this story doesn't end there – it explodes into mass-market consciousness. And this despite the fact that Arcade Fire would be known as 'the band with no hits', at least until the summer of 2011, when the subtle charms of

'Speaking In Tongues', complete with David Byrne's backing vocals, would drift down to mainstream radio across the globe, adding mass familiarity to the aura of this most gloriously awkward of bands.

Maybe we should have seen them coming? The past decade has seen vast changes in the very fabric of the music industry and, more pertinently, in the way in which the people in true control – those 17 year olds, lying on their beds, flicking through iPod tracks – explore music's rich history. The generation is the first that can cherry-pick their way through music's past by plucking individual tracks from classic albums. But even if they choose to consume an entire album from the iTunes store – Joy Division's *Unknown Pleasures* or The Smith's *The Queen Is Dead* perhaps – they still arrive at them with new ears in a state of time-shifted isolation. The music is not consumed in context, in the era or the environment or the circumstances in which it was created. This detachment changes the way the music sounds and is perceived, and these changes affect the listener and shift the balance of power away from the artist.

The two albums mentioned are, of course, creations of Manchester and this is deliberate. One could add Oasis' majestic, swaggering *Definitely Maybe*, the debut album by The Stone Roses or New Order's *Low Life*. These albums are all relevant here because of the immense influence they have had on this ungainly gaggle of serious musicians emerging shyly from the Montreal music scene in the early noughties,

"It is not just Manchester music… but I do think that was the key city for us," says a reflective Win Butler. "We spent so long listening to those records… songs of The Smiths and New Order and wondering about the environment in which they were created. We didn't really know much about Manchester. Still don't in many ways but it was important to know where they came from. It was important to understand why that music affected people in a certain way. Why it was loved and still is. That is music that somehow connects and seems to be part of a place and part of history. Kinda important to us. That is what we always wanted to achieve."

In purely musical terms, none of these albums contain anything like the legacy, the scope or density of Arcade Fire. In fact, and at last, here is a band that can be cherry-picked. For their music carries its own legacy that doesn't seem particularly rooted to Montreal. Indeed, a large part of its roots really do stretch back to the gloomy bedsits of Whalley Range in the early eighties – and lots of other places too.

Some are evocative, and sometimes for the wrong reasons. Arcade Fire's liking for performing at art galleries, house parties and lofts is not exactly the stuff of punk legend. There was no trolling up and down freeways in rusty Transits – or the Canadian equivalent – to perform in smoky clubs before a barrage of hostile inebriation. But it didn't seem to matter. Almost regardless of whether an audience was there or not, or how the audience behaved, Arcade Fire seemed happy to use performance as an act of rehearsal. In particular to hone a small collection of songs which, they felt, should be strong enough to catch the attention of an intelligent record label A&R man, and once they felt the songs were ready they made a series of demos, most of them during 'downtime' in any number of Montreal's eager and, more often than not, unused recording studios, backed by sessions in Win Butler's bedroom.

As such, the Arcade Fire EP was born.

Chapter 6

The Arcade Fire EP

Montreal offered little for Arcade Fire beyond eccentric house parties and gigs within a claustrophobic local scene that, while not without charm, showed little sign of opening any doors for their swelling ambition. Nevertheless, something remarkable was starting to happen in the practice room. Given the unusual scope of instrumentation, the initial set of Arcade Fire songs had started to develop into a general, all-encompassing 'sound', a fat and earth-shattering sound that fused all the influence of British indie rock, American metal, Americana, French Canadian, blues and bits of jazz, all mixed up into a solid wall of sound more often than not driven by a pulsating bass.

This sound certainly caused heads to turn at gigs, which perhaps wasn't surprising given the violas, violins and diverse percussive instruments not seen outside of folk festivals held way beyond the city limits. And while this emerging sound 'boomed' out in a way that suggested a pre-rock'n'roll hollow swing, it was brought fully up to date with a scattering of contemporary influences. More importantly, in a music world where for the convenience of radio programmers everything was divided into genre, no one else sounded quite like Arcade Fire.

This may explain why the sending of demos to record companies in Canada, the USA and England proved fruitless, which was disappointing to the band, but hardly surprising. The answer was to find a way of capturing the sound of Arcade Fire in a local studio. They now had several songs, so the idea took shape of making a mini album or expanded EP that might capture the scope and intensity that was being generated in their practice room in Montreal.

The EP, later to find acceptable remastered status and official release, became synonymous with the DIY nature of early Arcade Fire. While Win Butler would later scoff at this – "Huh. It *had* to be DIY... No one else was interested in us" – it offers an insight into the mindset of the band at this juncture. On their somewhat aloof trek through the small venues, art galleries, cafes and house parties of Montreal, Arcade Fire took great pains to sell the EP before and after their performances, often taking turns to mingle with punters and sell the CD on a one-to-one basis. There were times when this diligent sales ploy looked like it might become the future for the band; a sort of cottage industry launched with their own record label. It was without doubt the most obvious direction.

"We talked up a punk idealism," Win would later claim. "We certainly wondered if it could be done by ourselves."

Had this been five years later then the immense possibilities for self-promotion in the digital age might well have tempted the band to take that exact course of action, at least for the initial release – as in Arctic Monkeys – or in the actual formation of their own label as, say, Kate Rusby would achieve on the English folk circuit. Win Butler had also read of the earlier romantic absurdities of Manchester's Factory Records (placing the Durutti Column album in a sandpaper sleeve) and Buzzcocks (spending an afternoon at manager Richard Boon's house, physically placing their debut EP, 'Spiral Scratch', in its cheaply produced sleeve).

For a while, The Arcade Fire EP – briefly known as 'US KIDS KNOW EP' succeeded in achieving that romantic idyll. But it wasn't to last. The sheer scale of ambition that simmered within Win and Régine would surely see this EP used more as a lever to attract more serious record company action. As Win would later admit: "We were thinking big, really. For better or worse. I always saw us as a big band. I don't know whether that seems unethical to some people. But as a big band we could get the life we craved and also help a few people along the way."

The EP was released in November 2003, and opens with 'Old Flame'. If Arcade Fire had intended to produce one song that would encompass the scope and power of their new direction, a song that hints strongly at the intensity of their live show yet also contains a pointer to their future direction, then 'Old Flame' is surely the perfect choice. A powerful, driven rhythm section pushes the listener towards the song's heart, a soaraway keyboard that factors in the lighter moments of The Cure and New Order and, in addition, a dramatic sweeping back-echo that shimmers with anthemic promise. One listen is sufficient to convince that a future spent performing in big stadiums might surely beckon for this odd bunch of Montreal based mis-shapes.

Lyrically, the simple tale of letting go of an old love and finding solace in the idea that separation equals freedom probably doesn't warrant such anthemic backing, but this would soon become an Arcade Fire trait. Their ability to mine the sweeping and dramatic from everyday passions might seem like cracking a nut with a sledgehammer and on first listen it's certainly difficult to align a glorious, rousing melody with a line like, "Why do we go through all this shit again", the second appearance for this most ugly and regular of swear words. A clear case of setting out their stall, it is the manner in which the song rises from nothing and eventually collapses that is staggeringly effective.

'I Am Sleeping In A Submarine' is the first example of Arcade Fire's lyrical obsession with 'the neighbourhood', and it introduces the voice of Régine, lost in fifties pastiche. A themic song, it typifies Arcade Fire's desire to scrape under the surface of normality and find something subversive to sing about: the notion of normal life as 'a cage' and the desire to move on to a more fulfilling life. It is also a note to a lover about how frustrating is the attempt to move on. It is this frustration that explodes into the metaphorical surrealism: "I guess it's time to built a boat, make a raft of our bodies, do you think it'll float."

It is at once heartfelt and deliberately twee, and it reflects back to early days, especially as Win references Echo & the Bunnymen. "All hands on deck" recalls time spent musing over Ian McCulloch's mischievous lyrics on *Ocean Rain*. Butler noted, in *Spin* magazine: "I used to listen to Echo & the Bunnymen and marvel over the sheer courage of the lyrics. Some of them were plain bizarre but somehow Ian McCulloch got away with it and produced something that people clutched to their hearts. I knew that that is what I wanted to do. I learned a lot from listening to *Heaven Up Here* and *Ocean Rain* in particular. No one, as far as I could see, was writing music like that in America."

The track 'No Cars Go' is an initial recording of a simplistic existential statement – it would be revived later, on the *Neon Bible* album – and begins with the ticking of a clock and soon mounts to form a driving beat topped by an intrusive synthesizer whirr. It is a song of escape, a dream perhaps but, at least, an expression of a desire to depart the rat race. In this version – punkier and preferable to the later version, many say – Régine can be heard chanting in the background a gorgeous repetitive 'Dreams that click the light and the stars that dream' before the song settles to a crackling finale.

The band's dissatisfaction with the EP recording is difficult to fathom. It would return speeded up but without the edgy synth and lacking the spark and charm of this original recording,

'The Woodlands National Anthem' serves to emphasise the impact that life in Woodlands had on the young Butler brothers, for its silent leafiness and strange undercurrents would repeatedly bubble up lyrically across the first three Arcade Fire albums and flicker continually across over 30 songs. It might be said that the Woodland theme begins in earnest in this wry ditty, complete with wailing soul vocals and ironic handclaps. The song's funereal pace seems an odd kick-back from the driving beats that are the pulse of the rest of the EP and indicate that, at the point of writing, Win Butler may have merely wished to glance back to days of dreamy modernity.

As Arcade Fire made inroads into the Montreal music and art scene – via numerous appearances in house parties – 'My Heart Is An Apple' would become the proud centrepiece of their embryonic set. It is a beautiful song, a slow-paced scream with Win's vocals taking on an evocative heart-bellowing quality. It seems inconceivable that such a lovely echo of a song should begin with the line, "I'll admit I'm full of shit" (though, admittedly, it does rhyme) and follows through with the softer, "That's how I know I love you."

And it is a love song, too, effectively split into two halves and two lovers. When the song dissolves into the sounds of splashing through water, it is gratefully picked up by Régine, who concludes with "Please don't even call. I can't hear you at all."

'My Heart Is An Apple' lacks any kind of formulaic Arcade Fire 'sound' that might be forming and, indeed, is quite the reverse, its loose and fresh appeal pointing to a lost direction (unless they choose to pick up on it at some time in the future). That said, it is the first truly beautiful Arcade Fire song to find its way on record.

Whereas 'My Heart Is An Apple' will forever suggest an alternative direction for Arcade Fire, 'Headlights Look Like Diamonds' is the one track on the EP that completely and irrevocably points a way forward for any record company looking for a lucrative future direction. While the full-blown echoey blast that would become their signature noise – built as much from classical as rock formations – is only barely evident here, there is something about the driving, thrusting nature of 'Headlights Look Like Diamonds' that would have any potential producer salivating at the prospect of working with this remarkable young band. No doubt either that 'Headlights Look Like Diamonds' would echo strongly down the following three albums.

Lyrically it's about a paranoiac love affair that seems destined to end, with Win Butler relating his fears through the metaphor of a car journey in the rain. This itself is strongly reminiscent of Tom Waits' 'Diamonds On My Windshield' , from *The Heart Of Saturday Night*, an album that sat close to Win Butler's heart during his latter days at college. More tellingly perhaps, it contains the portentous line, "The suburbs are all sleeping"', which indicates that it is a tale of a love lost from Win's formative years. The importance of this seemingly throwaway line is barely noticeable within this context.

The final track, 'Vampire Forest Fire', is seven minutes long and stretches the old-fashioned concept of an EP to the limits. (Creedence Clearwater Revival would have called this a double album.) After all, 27 minutes had passed before reaching this epic, which uses simple mandolins and snare drum rim shots to build the band's trademark sound. All the drama is here, even if the production technique serves only to spread it rather thinly. Once again, it is a song that changes shape and resonance halfway through, a trick that would soon become as standard to Arcade Fire as the Edge's eerie guitar chops are to U2. Needless to say, the intensity builds significantly towards the end.

It is difficult to think of a single band in rock history that, following the release of such a tentative EP, was thrown into such a dizzying ascent. The comparison that most obviously springs to mind is that of Joy Division, back in 1978. They, too, emerged into the world with a self-financed EP, *An Ideal For Living*, which trickled out in initial 7-inch format before finding greater clarity and local penetration when later presented as a 12 inch. It was this release, accompanied by a string of stirring if ill-attended local gigs that caught the attention of Tony Wilson, then struggling with the kernel of an idea for a label he would call Factory.

Much has been made of both Arcade Fire's artistic links to Manchester – not least by the band themselves – and, indeed, a similar link between the innovative nature of both cities. But that, frankly, is where the story should end. For the Montreal rock scene, in 2003, was quite the antithesis of post-punk Manchester. Montreal, though bustling, bohemian and exciting, contained a huge number of musical artists, all competing for scant attentions in local, let alone national press.

However and despite these fundamental differences, a certain parallel between the two bands does emerge. Arcade Fire, like Joy Division, would skirt past the fleeting attentions of a major label, stay comparatively local and produce a genre-defying debut album that would not only tower above just about any release during its decade, but also power the label onto a completely different level, effectively changing the course of Montreal rock history.

It was, of course, unlikely that there was a label within the limited range of Arcade Fire that would have the vision, perception and sheer luck to be able to create a stir within the far more crowded market-place of 2003. Surely it would take a label driven by eclectic tastes and a desire to create a platform for artists that stood aside the irritatingly controlling norms of modern music genre. Did such a label really exist and, if so, what could it possibly be?

These were changing times in the music industry, and with major labels retreating hastily in fear of the oncoming rush of digital home recording and self-release, the prospect of signing a six-piece band to a major recording deal seemed unlikely, to say the least. In fact, and having conversed with a number of British record company A&R execs about this in recent months, they all agree that Arcade Fire managed to completely buck the prevailing trend. However exceptional their demo may have seemed, none of these A&R folk would have had the confidence to attempt to sell the prospect of a six-piece multi-instrumental unit of no recognisable genre to their bosses. Generally, the days of signing bands on multi-album deals and housing them in some residential studio for three months had become a thing of the past. Already, by 2003, the quick-return culture of the TV talent show was starting to make its distressing presence felt in the record industry. Marrying the winning singer with a producer and banging out the well-known cover they'd sung on TV guaranteed a hit album within three months. Increasingly, this rather depressing scenario was beginning to govern the music industry. What, therefore, were the chances of a band such as Arcade Fire? The logistics of recording them, or putting them on the road, was a nightmare. They were a band with no particular visual pull either. There was no certainty about where their own audience might lie, even if they had one. The figures did not stack up. In terms of identifiable commerciality, Arcade Fire managed to tick no boxes at all.

Win Butler was well aware of this huge problem – a problem that became all the more obvious when the rejection slips began to flow back with such dispiriting regularity.

Except for one, a label formed from the heady experience of one long-term band that had battled against prevailing trends to establish a foothold in the music industry. Their story stretches back to the summer of 1989 when Mac McCaughey and Laura Balance road-tripped with a crew of friends all the way from Durham, North Carolina, to Seattle, where a fledgling record label called Sub Pop was holding its first Lamefest where a largely unknown act called Nirvana would open for one of their favourite bands, Mudhoney. Mac's father's van caught fire en route, so they drove home from the festival in a rental car, without their friends.

Fired with passion for the music, and having not found a record label to support their own band, Superchunk*, they whiled away the long hours on the road talking about the label they would create for their own releases. Before they had even returned home they had discovered the name of this company – apparently taken from a road sign they noticed in the black night – Merge Records.

They also vowed, that night, that the label would maintain a true visionary stance and would not scuttle sheep-like after the latest trend, and that if they were successful enough to be in a position to sign artists, they would make that decision on the music alone. It will come as no surprise to discover that the label on which their ideal was built was the British label Rough Trade Records. So again it is no surprise that the two labels responsible for breaking Arcade Fire around the world would be Merge and, in Europe, Rough Trade.

In retrospect Arcade Fire might seem like rather an obvious signing – how many three-track demos contain songs of such quality? Equally importantly, Merge Records actually reported the power and strength of the live show, focusing on the 'possibilities' of the multi-instrumental format rather than stumbling over the logistical problems, both in terms of transporting and presenting the sound live and, frankly, sympathetically recording instruments such as the hurdy gurdy, flugelhorn and viola. It is notoriously difficult to capture the grey area that exists between classical orchestration and rock music, to use the complexity of the former and marry it with the latter. Somewhere, within that potential fog, a classic album lurked.

John Cook, writer of *Our Noise: The Story of Merge Records, the Indie Label That Got Big and Stayed Small,* noted to *Mother Jones* magazine: "There are a lot of moments in Merge's history when there's been

---

* Superchunk's measured success is perhaps a story not entirely relevant here, although, as this book was being written it was warming to see them still performing, not least as part of the bill for the 2011 All Tomorrow's Parties Festival at Butlins, Minehead. Eclectic to the last.

some serious urgency. When they're getting hit with records that were huge that they weren't expecting and they're freaking out trying to make sure the records get in the stores. But generally speaking, they're very Southern about the way they do things. Slow and considered, and without a lot of hoopla or noise – and Superchunk is fast and noisy, which is one of the great things about them."

Pensive in Austria. May 22, 2005, L to R: Sarah Neufeld, Win Butler, Regine Chassagne, Will Butler, Tim Kingsbury, Owen Pallett, Jeremy Gara, Richard Reed Parry. MICK HUTSON/REDFERNS

Win and William Butler's grandfather, Alvino Rey, a pioneer of the pedal steel guitar and leader of swing bands in America in the days before rock 'n' roll. MICHAEL OCHS ARCHIVES/GETTY IMAGES

Regine and Win photographed together in 2005. COLLEXXX · LEX VAN ROSSEN/REDFERNS

Richard Reed Parry of Arcade Fire during KROQ Inland Invasion 5 Show at Hyundai Pavilion at Glen Helen in Devore, California, 2005. JOHN SHEARER/WIREIMAGE

Composed. WENDY REDFERN/REDFERNS

The band listens to a poetry recital towards the end of a show at the Ukrainian Federation Hall in Montreal on February 10, 2007.
JOACHIM LADEFOGED/VII/CORBIS

About to launch *Neon Bible*, Arcade Fire on the mini-tour that takes them through Canada, New York and the most of Europe.
JOACHIM LADEFOGED/VII/CORBIS

Win Butler (L) in a pivotal performance at the Coachella Music Festival in Indio, California on April 28, 2007. MARIO ANZUONI/REUTER CORBIS

Arcade Fire rehearse backstage at the Coachella Festival at the Empire Polo Field in Indio, California on April 28, 2007.
KEVIN WINTER/GETTY IMAGES

One Regine Chassagne – two instruments in concert at Radio City Music Hall, New York, May 9, 2007. STARFACE/GREG ALLEN/ RETNA PICTURES

Win Butler and Regine Chassagne at the Glastonbury Festival, Britain, June 22, 2007. BRIAN RASIC/REX FEATURES

Regine on stage at the Hove Festival in Arundel, Norway, on June 27, 2007. GARY WOLSTENHOLME/GETTY IMAGES

Chapter 7

Funeral

At first glance – and first glances are so important, the marketing bods will stress – *Funeral* might not seem to be the most tantalising of album titles, nor perhaps the most enticing of concepts, either. Indeed, as a marketing concept, it would seem absurd to announce the arrival of a new major international band by invoking the ritual of death; wholly crass perhaps or at the very least the shallow ploy of some hardcore goth rock troupe formed in a Norwegian fjord, or somewhere significantly cold and unalluring. Funeral sounds like a shock tactic embellished with black, blood and roses.

It is a serious point. In an era when record companies are obliged to dumb down to the obvious in order to attract sales, to call a debut album *Funeral* and dress it in downer tones of brown, rather than sex it up in traditional black, red and white, would cause consternation in most record company boardrooms.

Mercifully for Arcade Fire, Rough Trade is not 'most' record companies. It has earned itself a reputation for encouraging iconic imagery from an organic source, the true heart of the band. The company has achieved this in spectacular fashion in the past by creating simple iconic visuals for artists' music, be it The Smiths, The Libertines, Lucinda Williams, Everything But The Girl or The Strokes. The best record companies understand that, even if they don't know it themselves, most bands are their own best graphic designers.

Funeral might not have seemed like an easy sell, especially in a market in a state of nervous downturn, but it was Arcade Fire themselves who arrived at this grey and misty concept by using the most basic materials and emotions they could find. Indeed, the very reason they – and 'they' may be Will and Régine or, indeed, the whole band and a few bit part players beyond – arrived at the concept was on purely artistic grounds. For Will, Régine and Richard Reed Parry, who constituted the songwriting heart of Arcade Fire, had all suffered the very real pain as a result of the death of a close relative in the years leading up to the writing of the songs that would make up *Funeral*.

Régine's grandmother passed away in June 2003. In March of the following year, the Butler brothers lost their grandfather and, within a month of that sad and significant passing, Richard Parry's aunt passed away too.

The timings are immensely significant in that the bulk of the songs destined for the *Funeral* sessions would be written by those deeply affected by these losses. Both Régine and Win have stated that they allowed their state of mind to affect the course of the songwriting. In effect, it was more than that. Funerals are curiosities of Western contemporary life, fleeting occasions when the bereaved are obliged to confront emotions that society prefers to keep at bay. Few mourners arrive at funerals with a solid understanding of what is actually happening to them. Death, as natural and beautiful as birth, lies hidden from general understanding. When it arrives, and when a funeral cortege arrives at a church, a strange and sorrowful simplicity prevails; a simplicity that, for most mourners, will have been lost since childhood. It is the most basic and pure emotion of all.

Win Butler: "I became aware, through the process of the funeral, that I was somehow touching something that had been lost. I spoke at length with Régine and we both felt the same."

As tragic as the funerals were, for Win, Régine and Richard they also presented a unique opportunity to bring out the natural aesthetic, the gatherings of family and friends providing a rich, colourful and powerful web of emotion, with people lost in memories of loved ones and an acknowledgement of their uniqueness.

Régine: "There is no doubt that being at a funeral provides you with such a valuable connection to the things that are most important and this is truly inspirational... well it certainly was for us. That experience started a huge rush of creativity. It seemed to enrich us."

Inspirational and enriching are not words that normally spring to mind when considering funerals, yet in modern culture, most notably films – *Gone To Earth, The Godfather, Control* – they are portrayed as moments of fleeting poignancy rather than inspiration.

Win: "We wanted to look beyond that regular idea of the funeral being merely a full stop. There is much more to it than that. They are important events and we can learn a great deal from them."

Built into this, of course, is an element of catharsis. All art of any real worth is born from some kind of pain, be it love or loss or a sense of feeling distanced from the wheels of society in general. The artist attempts to create a way through it, to make sense of it all. But with a funeral, there are other considerations, the deep strands of family and the many loves and altercations that are so peculiarly tangled. And just as important, it would seem, is the placing of all this family history and pain that is lost in a rather featureless environment, often described by Arcade Fire as a 'neighbourhood' or, in a later album, as *The Suburbs*. These vague landscapes are more than backcloth, despite their apparently desolate and emotionless appearance. This is the true canvass of Arcade Fire.

Funeral could have been called 'Songs Of Love And Death' or, more inelegantly, 'Songs Of Love, Death, Pain, Grief, Illness And The Rediscovery Of Childlike Innocence All In A Place Called The Neighbourhood.'

Or it could just have been called 'Nowhere'. Or 'Neighbourhood'.

The opening song on *Funeral*, 'Neighborhood 1 (Tunnels)', would serve as the introduction to Arcade Fire for millions around the world. It was grandiose enough to encapsulate the very essence of their sound, their feeling, their vast musical scope and depth, all dipped into the eeriness of a funeral. A song destined to open a set at some vast arena, or many vast arenas, it carried the message that Arcade Fire's sound is a vast arena, full of drama and emotion. It all begins with a soft humming organ, lilting strings and a pianist fixed in stoic repetition, then this sweet innocence is blasted away by the pulsatingly dark sexuality of the incoming bass.

What a perfect way, therefore, to create a cinematic opening blast and introduce the voice of Win Butler to the world. His voice is at once fevered and edgy, full-throttle and emotive as if describing some traumatic incident. He is in character. A young man deserting his weeping parents, escaping with the girlfriend he secretly met in the town square, together they are planning some kind of future, swept along by the energy of youth, the credulous uncertainty of their joint future and the blur of a young and barely formed love. The song sees the couple growing old, moving into an increasingly surreal world, perhaps in illness, where they look back to the lives they once led with their parents. It is, at once, quite gloriously bleak and powerfully sexual and, even though it concludes with a deathly metaphor, it seems to offer some kind of hope as the heart prevails beyond the final act of scattering the ashes.

Phew! By this time there are no casual listeners. Even if the fuzzed lyricism escapes your ears, you will be in no doubt that the album – and indeed, the career that is to follow – is not going to be '20 Party Hits'. This is an album heavier than the sharpest metal and blacker than the goths that gather in Yorkshire parks.

A theme that would come to typify Arcade Fire – suburban alienation, existentialism from the soft estates, perhaps – is introduced in the following track, 'Neighborhood 2 (Laika)'. This is a middle-class song, born from the boredom of days – perhaps when sick – spent lost in the silence of suburbia, where the sheer weight of unswerving normality starts to twist the mind into something quietly sinister. The alienation slowly encourages suicidal tendencies and, at least, the desire to escape such normality... or such a life.

Despite this soon-to-become trademark theme, 'Neighborhood 2' is an unlikely anthem, as it remains locked solid within a traditional rock structure, not the likeliest place for an Arcade Fire song to reside. Despite these conventional walls, 'Neighborhood 2 (Laika)' still manages to sustain the grey surrealism of the opening song, and so can be seen as a continuum. Rather like those 'Part Two' affairs so fashionably aired in the late sixties (Fleetwood Mac's 'Oh Well', Derek & The Dominoes' 'Layla'), it serves as a counterbalance without reacting against the lyrical flow.

'Une Année Sans Lumiere' sees an interesting departure, evoking a different location entirely. Forget the eerie silence of the metaphorical neighbourhoods, here is a beautiful and haunting snapshot of Win Butler's Montreal. Strips of streetlights and floating headlights shimmer in the night and the dreaming protagonist is swept aside as the song explodes into a frenzy of urban life, a clamour and scamper, as cold faces zip past in the rush hour. There is a perfect blend of old and new here, which echoes neatly back to a lost Montreal, a city of hope and possibility. As the clatter explodes, the urban tumult is both exhilarating and sadly disrespectful of the past. It's quite a perfect illustration of a song that seeks to illustrate the downside of a modern lifestyle and prove, if proof were needed, that Win Butler's songwriting prowess was maturing at an extraordinary rate. Not since the musically naïve Joy Division had hit their unlikely rush of creativity in the late seventies has a band developed at such an extraordinary rate. Unlike Joy Division, who in their early days were encumbered by a lack of musical skills, Arcade Fire benefitted from a vast and colourful musical template and, indeed, the ability to fully realise the potential of their aesthetic ambition. There are downfalls to such realised musicianship, not least a tendency to over-elaborate, to 'show off' in the manner of progressive rock bands from the early seventies who shall remain nameless (but the guilty parties know who they are). Thus far, Arcade Fire have managed to rein in such urges, producing a depth of sound that retains a pleasing simplicity yet leaves no doubt in the mind that those who are performing it know their way around their instruments.

The third in the album's sequence of 'Neighborhood' songs, 'Neighborhood 3 (Power Out)' offers the first iconic flashes of Arcade Fire. In England, a bombastic appearance on *Later With Jools Holland* seemed to instantly confer cult status on the group, encapsulating as it did the virtuosity and power of the band's live performance. Arguably the most performance-friendly song in the band's repertoire to date, it is fairly simple, pulsating and blessed with chanting tub-thumping vocals that, once heard, are difficult to forget. Thrilling changes of tempo are built into the song and allow members of the group to switch instruments to playfully alter the onstage dynamic, building the song towards an audacious climactic flurry, and then another one, and another one. The vocal is pushed to the edge of sheer exasperation and, in that state, Butler's character enigmatically chants, "I went out into the night, I went out to pick a fight… with anyone," a seemingly subversive outburst that describes a state of anarchic abandonment. This is a post personal–apocalypse song, when the world has come crashing down and there is nothing left but a resounding state of fury and damn the consequences.

'Power Out' quickly came to be regarded as the album's gargantuan centrepiece, its mesmeric chopping guitars and hypnotic pounding turning it into what was arguably the first great rock anthem of the 21st century, and firmly cementing Arcade Fire's image in the minds of those who turned a sympathetic ear in their direction. Now there was no doubt that this band would be 'big' in every conceivable way. Big, big, big tune and infectious post-rage wind-down, providing Régine with the perfect opportunity for onstage theatrics, her gloved hands clawing to the top at the song's heartfelt conclusion.

Beyond the wrath of 'Power Out's bombast lay the fourth 'Neighborhood' song, 'Neighborhood 4 (7 Kettles)', a startling and immediate drop down to a squeaky acoustic guitar delivering a touch of unlikely acid folk. Its post-apocalyptic visions making it the first true surprise on the album, the lilting vocals relate dark tales about where suburban families take control and burn the 'old folks, the witches and the liars', the flames 'getting hotter' as the song builds, slowly gathering intensity. Then, with a resigned air, Butler's character starts to contemplate a new green future, where motor cars no longer roam and food is something you grow. His decision is to look for love no more but, if only metaphorically, sow a seed and give it time to grow. The mood is contemplative rather than explosive, all the anger seemingly drained away and all that remains are thoughts and vague notions of a new kind of future. The battle is over.

Just when you think it safe to wander through acoustic pastures, in comes 'Rebellion (Lies)', another thunderous anthem, complete with the – increasingly – trademark hypnotic chanting. "Every time you close your eyes, lies," chirp in the entire band at the song's conclusion. Before that they exhort us not to give in to sleep patterns, to remain awake and fight. The message is the age-old urge to fight for what you believe in and not allow 'them' to overcome and over-rule, a cry to not submit to mightier earthly powers, and to at least retain a vital streak of individualism.

Like 'Power Out', the song would soon find its way into the heart of the band's live set. It also featured as a showcase song in the film of the 1994 Coachella festival, held deep in the California desert. Amid Radiohead, Oasis, The Stooges and White Stripes came this strangely charismatic tribe with their full-on quasi-religious gesticulations and moments of blissed-out intensity. Even on a bill that included The Flaming Lips, who are pretty much adrift on their own planet, no other band seemed so distant from the tradition and drudgery of the sort of rock personified by the Gallagher brothers. Even Radiohead, by comparison, seemed rather drawn and obvious.

'Crown Of Love', which follows, is a different landscape altogether. At first listen, it is a rolling hills and gentle weather kind of a song, wherein the softness of Win Butler's voice is backed by soaring strings, distant backing vocals and a plod, plod, plodding of drum and viola. The song gathers pace but, until its violent upheaval four minutes in – when it becomes a chugging slap of hot funk before fading weirdly – it always feels like the kind of exit music intended to make you leave a cinema in an altered state, even if you are merely walking through a multiplex car park in Doncaster. So it is with 'Crown Of Love' which, in terms of the music, is all about heightened awareness and senses working overtime.

Despite this, 'Crown Of Love' provides the darkest moments of an already dark album. Superficially a steady-paced ballad, the lyrics drive you into a despairing expression of lovesick guilt and a man wrestling with the ferocious power of that basic emotion. There seems no exit from this psychological wrestling, either as the song drives deeper and deeper into the depths of that despair until that funky conclusion arrives like a blessed angel or masturbatory relief, whichever way you wish to take it.

'Wake Up', on the other hand, goes up like a kite. How many anthems can one album take? Despite all that had gone before, no one will ever forget the first time they heard 'Wake Up', the most gloriously bedecked song on the album and the perfect counter-balance to the heavy heart of the previous track. It is gorgeously drawn, too, with long stretched vocals pulled tight across the most uplifting pseudo-evangelical backing in modern music.

A song about growing awareness and learning how to face death full in the face, its basic lyrical twist aims at the lie of life that we teach to children, the inference being that it is best to allow children to grow up in the knowledge that life will become colder and that early promise is unlikely to last forever. "Children, wake up," pleads Win, "before they turn the summer into dust."

The realisation that "the rainstorm is turning every good thing to rust" is not, however, delivered with any sense of despair. Indeed, this is a brightly coloured powerhouse of a song that lifts magnificently in several places before sprouting out into a jaunty hop that might initially seem misplaced if not rather flippant. Only when Régine weighs in with images of "lightning bolts a-glowin'" does the song regain its depth. In the end it becomes more frantic as she screams a concluding "You had better look out below" as, indeed, a lightning bolt crashes into the song's defiant tail, cutting short what is arguably the finest song on the album, if not of the band's entire career to date.

For 'Haiti', inevitably, Régine steps up to the mic. Suddenly her entire demeanour has darkened. Gone is the bouncing fizz-bomb on the stage. She stares intently into space while punching out the lyrics, half English, half French, her bare arms reaching forward and beginning a cycle motion as she arrives at the heart of the song. This is her song, her lyrics, her family, her country. It is steeped in the political atrocities that had blighted her country and caused her family to flee, delivering her at a place where she can build and scream back.

The song recalls the atrocities committed by the paramilitaries called The Tonton Macoutes who, serving the evil Duvaliers, terrorised their own people for decades. The French lines are not delivered in formal French language but in a Haitian dialect, which pulls the song to her chest, making it an incredibly personal statement: "My cousins never bore, the haunted nights of Duvalier, nothing can our spirits decree, guns can't kill what soldiers can't see."

Perhaps deliberately, it is impossible to translate the song accurately, as two stanzas in French end perfectly but become awkward when translated. I like to think this is to the song's benefit as half of it seems all the better for having been delivered in that particularly evocative dialect. That stated, the grandiose nature of the song offers a universal message, its heartfelt lyrics of tearful defiance echoing the conflicts against repressive regimes anywhere in the world. It is not a song of revenge – although this would be perfectly understandable – but of indomitable spirit that will always triumph over guns and grenades, and the cold hearts of those who blindly wield them.

It is also a song of startling beauty, green, rain-soaked and steaming, a whole island of emotion.

The album's closing song, 'In The Backseat', is well-nigh perfect. Régine's voice drifts over violins and piano, intoning a faintly sinister tale of watching a life come to a grinding halt. The song explodes into violent emotion, grinding, masculine guitars clashing horribly with a voice that refuses to change. The track deepens to a satanic red, and one imagines all kinds of raging fury, crowds hurtling through the night, couples lost in domestic argument, warring countries and political opposites, before a swirl of violins lift the song from the depths of mayhem, plucking away and putting the album firmly to sleep. It is an unsettling closer and probably not a track that commands too many hits on the selector. Why conclude so unhappily, perhaps to leave a promise hanging in the air? The harshness of 'In The Backseat' leaves a large gaping silence that Régine can fill in the future.

In a decade where classic, genre-defying albums remain conspicuous by their absence, *Funeral* stands unique, proud and gloriously aloof. This alone might be enough to attain 'classic status' but as it arrived during an era which saw a welcome re-emergence of, for want of a better word, 'Americana', a number of critics were tempted to categorise it thus. This appallingly lazy pigeonholing doesn't stand up to scrutiny at all. For Arcade Fire would seem to have little in common with check-shirted, bickering boyo brothers – Kings of Leon – or beardy waifs and strays who prefer the ambience of log cabins in woods, lakes and bears. A vague strand can be traced back from such bands – Decemberists, Fleet Foxes, Midlake – to days when Canned Heat's evocative if juvenile country-blues shone so effectively from the Woodstock soundtrack. Closer, perhaps, might be the link to the great Tom Waits – and, beyond him, Tim Buckley – wherein elements of blues, country, folk, rock and swamp are fused confusingly into the backdrop of the artists' distinctive urban poetry.

That, of course, is where Waits – a man relishing the tough edge of town – and the Butler Brothers – so profoundly from the middle-class suburbs – might seem to depart. But built into *Funeral* are other distant echoes that arguably push the album closer to *Pilgrim's Progress* than any comparable rock act. The album exists as a heady historical trip through the avenues of American history wherein lie campfire cowboy songs, fairground music, mountain and canyon echoes, deep rooted sexual blues of the south and ardent religious tub-thumping. In fact, the church and, in particular, the darkest reaches of weird American churches, remain so solidly built into the Arcade Fire ethos that it is surprising to note that no known conspiracy theories followed in its wake. Is this the dark side of Christianity pushing into the rock arena? Well, Win Butler has never attempted to hide his fascination with the Bible or with all religion as a subject for research. Of course that doesn't make him a believer and, even if it did, why would that necessarily be a bad thing. (Fans of U2 and Evanescence might like to chip in here.) Not since, I suggest, Brian Wilson's infamous *Smile*, which found eventual release 30 years after its partial completion, has a record managed to grasp the wide scope of American music to such poignant effect. Americana perhaps, but in a truer sense of the word than its backwoods connotations.

Funeral is its own genre. Whether Arcade Fire would choose to remain within its powerful outline remained to be seen. One thing was certain, no other band even glimpsed over this horizon before.

Funeral was arguably the most significant breakthrough album of the decade. Awards and record-breaking statistics trailed in its wake, and it is important to focus on these in order to grasp just how this collection of gargantuan songs managed to defy all manner of record industry convention. Less than a handful of albums in any recent decade could be said to have achieved this kind of success which scattered like an ever expanding fan of dominoes, quite literally around the globe.

The success was staggered only because of delayed international release schedules. Feverishly snatched by Rough Trade in 2005, *Funeral* took its place alongside groundbreaking releases such as The Libertines' *Up The Bracket* and The Strokes' *Is This It*, subsequently helping to steady the esteemed company's books and push it towards a new level. It is significant also that Arcade Fire's breakthrough came at the precise moment when the record industry began to fragment due to the explosion of digital record files and the consequent ease and speed with which music could be relayed from the bedroom to a global audience, or shared between its aficionados. Because of this, the record industry was in a state of swift and mass retreat. And here was a band capable of brushing such fears aside by the simple force and distinctive nature of their music.

Funeral moved smoothly into top ten lists across America, and then across the world. In the States, at the end of a tumultuous year for US music, the influential websites of Pitchfork, No Ripcord and Filter *all* named it Album of the Year, and while this might not seem to be as prestigious as winning a Grammy, it is actually a better measure of true worth. Many albums from big-selling and established artists gain huge sales within the first few weeks before tailing off thereafter. *Funeral* reversed this trend, its sales growing steadily from the date of release. Since it was a debut album by a largely unknown act this was only natural, but its solid, steady growth indicated that it was the idiosyncratic power of the music that sold – as opposed to the celebrity or otherwise of the artists who produced it.

In England, in 2005, the situation was similar. It claimed second place in *NME*'s Album of the Year listing with 'Rebellion (Lies)' claiming Second Best Song. Again, that might not seem all-conquering, although it should be noted that *NME*'s readership would not naturally be drawn towards a band such as Arcade Fire.

Perhaps the most startling statistic, given the lack of resources at Merge Records for a release of such magnitude – they could not do much in the way of promotion, especially when it came to TV advertising – was that sales figures pushed towards 750,000 within the first year of release. This was large enough to usurp Neutral Milk Hotel's *In The Aeroplane Over The Sea* as the label's biggest-selling artist to date. It even saw the label making its debut in the *Billboard* 200 chart.

The album also had an immense impact on the band and their lives. Firstly, its success took them completely by surprise. Immediately after its release, using a local promotions company, they embarked on a lengthy string of dates, initially in Canada and the US but stretching into Europe by 2005. The basic idea was to work themselves slowly towards the next level, stepping up their already established work-rate and beginning at the small end of the venue scale. It was a tactic born of wisdom – filling small venues creates a greater impact than failing to fill larger ones. When this started to cause major problems the venues were happily changed and, as 2005 dawned, included several festival appearances – Coachella, California, Leeds UK and Ireland's Electric Picnic – which we will focus on later – among them.

The escalation from dingy club to major festival attraction in such a short space of time was astounding. The immediate effect was an expansion of their onstage theatricals, bringing in elements of pseudo-ecclesiastical fervour, mind control and hysteria, all of which offered a new area of release and an opportunity for each individual member to develop their onstage persona. This was most obvious with Régine, whose charismatic shadow dancing would become a powerful and central feature of the live performance. Win, who until now was the sole visual persona in the band, affected a subtle retreat to allow more room for the others. In short, it was in the wake of *Funeral*, that the Arcade Fire performance became a show. This in itself served to speed up sales, and increase the all-round fervour. By accident, Arcade Fire had evolved into a sellable international live unit, festival favourites in no time at all and fast moving towards the major international arenas. Not bad for a band who, just one year earlier, were performing at house parties.

The media responded to full effect, drafting in high-profile writers to pen larger, deeper and more revealing portraits. The initial breakthrough was when they were featured as the cover story on *Time* magazine, albeit the Canadian edition, in April 2005. This served merely to emphasise the band's apparent shyness when faced with revealing much about themselves in an interview. Indeed, time after time, it was this act of retreat that would become the focus of the article. No wonder. Why would a band that has worked so hard to achieve such immense success recoil swiftly when faced with even mildly probing questions? The answer evidently lay within the strength of their camaraderie. They adopted a powerful gang-like mentality, and while this served to increase the enigmatic pull of the band, it also caused a ripple of concern as they acquired a reputation for 'stand-offishness'.

Régine Chassagne: "After a performance I just need to retreat. I don't wish to get into conversations with people I don't know. It's not that I do not appreciate that they are enthusiastic… but I don't really know them and I can't do that false smile thing."

This became part of their modus operandi, not just their constant retreat from fan adoration but their aversion to, and distrust of, record industry sycophancy. The bigger the band became, the more the industry's movers and shakers gather for post-gig 'meet-and-greets'. More often than not, when faced with these intrusions, the band would disperse back to their hotels or the sanctuary of quiet restaurants. Intriguingly, as reports of this indifference started to filter more frequently into the media, it did little to damage their reputation in the eyes of fans. Here was a major band that had absolutely no truck with the increasingly powerful cult of celebrity. Arcade Fire had never been celebrities and, even though they are omnipresent in the world's music media, never will be. They are simply not cut from that cloth and interviews, even the best of them, do little to discover their true heart.

Despite this sense of retreat, and much to the relief of Merge, which was beginning to realise exactly what it had on its hands by this stage, the band permitted their music to be used in selected television adverts ('Rebellion (Lies)' and 'Neighborhood (Tunnels)' both featuring lucratively on US commercials. While debates about such nakedly commercial publishing moves may have split the opinion of the more high-minded among fans, it certainly helped to address the problem of lack of television exposure due to the Merge budget constraints.

Having suddenly achieved what looked like a seemingly permanent place in rock's gilded hierarchy, Arcade Fire now found themselves offered 'opening slots' for all manner of rocks acts who were, perhaps, keen to be seen pledging allegiance to the critical hipness that had started to surround the band. Cynical as this may seem, there is no doubt that kudos could be gained by association. Not, I hasten to add, that U2 would harbour anything more than a new-found love of the band's music when they took Arcade Fire on tour towards the end of 2005. As newly celebrated local heroes the group were supporting U2 in hockey arenas. They were on form, and when Arcade Fire are on form, keen as hell, forced by time, lost in music, determined to prove themselves, taking the bull by the horns, breaking the ice, spreading good cheer, saving souls, storming the barricades and putting on a show that can destroy cynicism, they're the one group in the world that can match, even transcend, the battling spirit and sincerity of U2. You could also put them on a bill with the ripest Bruce, the deadliest Dylan, the heaviest Joy Division and the moodiest Roxy and they could hold their heads high and march toward glory, and possibly, as if there is still such a thing in this neighbourhood, history. U2 tried to persuade Arcade Fire to join them as they continued their world tour, one that was to visit Japan, South America and Australia, and end a few months later in Hawaii. It was a tempting offer, and Bono used his most overly persuasive powers to convince the group to come with them. "I wouldn't want any other group to support us ever again," enthused an infatuated Bono.

The group, though, had their own plans. Flushed with the success of *Funeral* and keen to explore elements of ambient recording, they decided to look at the prospect of purchasing a church, somewhere in the Montreal area, and transforming it into a studio with living accommodation. They were on the lookout for a building that could become the perfect manifestation of the sound they started on *Funeral*. To this most extraordinary of bands, this seemed a perfectly natural move. Indeed, to plough their sudden rush of money into bricks, mortar and ecclesiastical inspiration, seemed, at once, the most sensible and exciting way forward. But first they had to find the building.

Among the many allies that Arcade Fire attracted as the idea of becoming professional musicians became a viable career option was Owen Pallett who was active on the Montreal and Toronto scene throughout the first decade of the 21st century, and blessed with a musical background so effortlessly apt it would have seemed weird had he not ended up as at least a part-time member of Arcade Fire. Despite that lack of full membership, his input has been, and remains, a vital cog in this peculiar machinery.

On the fringe of full Arcade Fire membership since the recording of *Funeral*, Pallett remains better known for his extraordinary career both as a solo artist, producer, session musician and musical arranger. It is this latter role, orchestrating the string arrangements in conjunction with the rest of the band, that has seen him evolve as integral to the creation of that 'sound', while never quite becoming a full band member. Nevertheless, there is no doubt that Pallett's vision is deeply ingrained within the fabric of the band. He reminds me, slightly, of ex-Magazine bassist Barry Adamson, a musician who fitted so perfectly into the general vision of the band while simultaneously feeling slightly stifled within the band environment.

Michael James Owen Pallett was born in September, 1979, in Toronto. His father was a church organist who took great pains to teach his son the principles of music theory before teenage years distracted his attention span. The young Pallett seized this opportunity eagerly, studying classical violin and composing his first violin-based piece of music at the age of 13. Before leaving college he had composed two full operas as well as supplying background soundtracks for computer games. On leaving college he found himself commissioned by the Vancouver CBC Orchestra.

Pallett's entry into indie music came via the name Final Fantasy. Using this moniker he recorded 'Have A Good Home' in 2005, which was released by Blocks Recording Club, a Toronto–based collective of which he was a founding member. It was a clever and perfect way to make a mark, if only locally, and set his career in motion. Using his own name he released two further albums, *He Poos Clouds* in 2005 and the critically acclaimed *Heartland* in 2010. By this time, of course, Pallett had gained greater credence via his extensive work with Arcade Fire. In addition there have been a series of singles and EPs, again critically well received even if they failed to seriously trouble charts or gain much radio play.

His further collaborations include a spell in the now defunct Toronto three-piece Les Mouches, playing fiddle with the badly named Celtic outfit, Enter The Haggis, and keyboard duties for SS Cardiacs. He has also worked with The Last Shadow Puppets, Beirut and Picastro.

Of particular interest here is his song 'This Is The Dream Of Win And Régine', inspired by his work as string arranger on *Funeral* and the forthcoming *Neon Bible*. In 2007, without his permission, the song was used in a commercial for Wiener Stadtwerke*. While most artists would have instructed their lawyers to enter into messy litigation over something like this, Pallet instead went into lateral thought mode and cleverly suggested that the company provide sponsorship for the

---

* Austrian energy distribution company Wiener Stadtwerke did initially approach Owen Pallett under his Final Fantasy guise, and asked if it could use 'This Is The Dream Of Win And Régine' in a television commercial. Pallett, finding no obvious link with the company, declined. This failed to deter the company who used a cover version of the song which included different violin parts and a male vocal asking "Can you feel it?" The song was duly credited to something or someone called N.A.S.C.O. It was at this point that Owen Pallett asked for financial help for the festival. Why the company was so determined to use the tune in the first place remains unclear.

Maximum Black Festival in which he was involved both as curator and artist, performing as Final Fantasy.

Given the extraordinary scope and depth of his musical adventures, it seems inconceivable that he would have even found the time and space to become integral to the Arcade Fire sound. However, integral he remains, contributing heavily to the ecclesiastical atmosphere to be found within the band's music. Without Owen Pallett, Arcade Fire would be a different and a lesser beast.

Chapter 8

Are You Ready World?

The CMJ Music Marathon and Film Festival seems to sit at the very heart of the left-field cultural life of New York City. Although broad in spectrum, in terms of music, film and other related art forms it provides the perfect showcase 'shop window' for breaking rock acts, projecting them directly into the heart of New York's famous music cognoscenti. One successful performance at CMJ is enough to guarantee a band a large and influential following in the city. It also serves to attune broadsheet music writers to an artist's potential.

At the 2004 event, the post-*Funeral* Arcade Fire might have seemed to be too big for the loose term 'showcase', although their set was so spectacularly successful that Manhattan city dwellers were talking about it for weeks afterwards and local sales of *Funeral* simply went through the roof. This surprised many, for Arcade Fire did not appear on the surface to be a 'New York kind of group', given the parochial nature of their music and image, although a hearty endorsement from Lou Reed and collaborations with David Byrne certainly helped matters.

Arcade Fire returned to the CMJ Music Marathon and Film Festival in 2005, by this time a thoroughly established global act and, without doubt, the true stars of the event. They performed on the second night of the four-day event amid a general celebratory air. After all, their steep ascent had seen their collective lifestyles alter to dramatic effect. This meant comparatively effortless travelling, the tedium being softened considerably by the luxurious comforts of first-class flying, five-star hotels and all the forelock-tugging attention that followed them around, seemingly 24-7. Of course, Arcade Fire being what they are – what they aren't are standard goofy rock stars willing to soak up all manner of sycophantic attention – they approached the entire year with a determination to distance themselves from the more unwelcome forms of attention, from over-inquisitive journalists to over-enthusiastic fans.

Of course, this works both ways. Stars they may have become, but that doesn't mean that they, too, couldn't feel a little awestruck when their own heroes started to gravitate towards them offering unsolicited compliments. In short, Arcade Fire had found little difficultly in attracting the rock glitterati.

Although used to this by now, the attentions of David Bowie during the week leading up to the second CMJ performance were accepted with good grace from the band who – pushing their own sense of awe aside – found the man to be utterly charming, peculiarly down-to-earth and fired with many enthusiasms that they eagerly shared. In short, they seemed to enjoy very similar musical tastes which, more often than not, drifted towards the eclectic (Deerhoof, Polyphonic Spree, Air etc). Two years later, while curating the High Line Festival in the same city, Bowie would use the skills he honed at London's Meltdown in 2002 to assemble all these acts and more – and Arcade Fire, in what became a general celebration of idiosyncratic rock talent from the previous 10 years. It was Bowie's seemingly unbridled enthusiasm and surprising knowledge of breaking acts from around the world, plus his ability to focus on the more interesting ones, that fired the imaginations of the various members of Arcade Fire.

On stage, that night, Win Butler strode briskly to the mic, flicked his hair from across his left eye and announced: "This one is a David Bowie song." According to Bowie biographer Mark Spitz, "Three thousand cell-phone cameras were thrust into the air as Butler strummed the opening chords to 'Queen Bitch'."

It was a good choice, and a fine tribute; instantly recognisable and not the most obvious of Bowie songs to perform, even if its rudimentary block chords were not entirely attuned to the more sophisticated instrumentation of Arcade Fire. Nevertheless, it seemed apt, being a song strongly influenced by the tough streets of downtown Manhattan and written in respect to Lou Reed who had so perfectly captured New York's lowlife with The Velvet Underground.

Then came Bowie, resplendent in a white suit, smiling freely, grasping the mic stand, spitting out the opening line: "I'm up on the eleventh floor and I am watching the cruisers below." All too easy to imagine it was Lou Reed, standing there, proud to front this most evocative of contemporary acts. And as he sang, the band looked on with wonderment crossing their features. How did this happen? How did they get from student digs to playing on stage with one of their all-time heroes? More than that, actually sharing mutual respect with the man who, halfway through a song written 10 years before Butler was born, was clearly thoroughly enjoying himself.

In his book, *David Bowie, A Biography*, Spitz suggests that Bowie saw something personal in Arcade Fire, that they reminded him of his own "… Bohemian strum sessions in suburban Beckenham at the end of the sixties… The Arcade Fire's gear, with its scratches and stickers, had the look and feel of such musty, smoke-cured ad hoc studios."

This period immediately prior to Arcade Fire directing their attention to their 'difficult' second album – a rock cliché that has grown increasingly ominous in recent times, as The Kaiser Chiefs, Glasvegas, Duffy, Joss Stone and the Klaxons would come to testify – saw them attracting the full force of rock glitterati. At the epicentre however, it would be churlish to accept that anything less than a genuine fire would be rekindled in the hearts of the elder statesmen. This seemed particularly intense in New York, where the attentions of royal rock personages such as Lou Reed and David Byrne were not to be sniffed at.

In the midst of all this spiralling success, in May 2005, Arcade Fire signed a short-term publishing deal with EMI, effectively elevating them into the big league, hence those television advertisements. A short-term contract would not provide enormous cash advance but it would allow the band and their London-based management the option to readdress their position one year down the line. It was a simple commonsense approach which allowed the best of both worlds and, as things were beginning to happen at a staggering rate, and with no actual guarantee that this explosion of success would continue, it seemed the way forward. The band were mindful that they would soon be approaching that tricky area of the 'difficult' second album, which had triggered extraordinary disappearances of acts with huge-selling debut albums over the years. Sustaining success is where the true money lies. Without that, then the initial blast of money soon runs into the negative.

Of course, with the full force of EMI on their side, doors of all shapes and sizes started to fling themselves open. For the most part, Arcade Fire strode briskly through. A new single, 'Cold Wind', was released via inclusion in the television series *Six Feet Under* (Volume II, *Everything Ends*). The link with David Bowie was furthered on the TV special *Fashion Rocks* (September 9, 2005) in which the Bromley Boy contributed accompanying vocals to 'Wake Up'. EMI's deft hand also eased this recording, alongside the band's versions of two Bowie standards – 'Life On Mars' and 'Five Years' – onto iTunes as a virtual live EP. At this precise moment came a legendary appearance on the hugely influential *Late Show With David Letterman*, always a sure sign that the US audience had woken up to a band's charms. To the band's utter delight, they also hurtled through a bombastic concert in New York's Central Park, again featuring a surprise appearance from Bowie, with all band members seemingly in awe of a new-found status that recalled gargantuan events such as the Simon & Garfunkel reunion concert.

"It defies belief," admitted Win Butler. "You find yourself wondering if it is a dream or a film. Then you start to wonder why you don't really feel any different, having gained the one thing you always strived for. It's not really a disappointment. We are not 'starry' people so, in some ways, it is a relief to be hurled into this mad pace of life and yet still have large amounts of boredom and angst. Just like everyone else. Success does *not* change that. I think we all realised at the same time that life would not suddenly become this wonderful glowing existence. It wouldn't basically change at all, other than giving us the chance to carry on making and playing music. That's all we ever wanted."

Over in England, where the long-running chart show *Top Of The Pops* was edging into its final phase, the band mimed hilariously through 'Rebellion (Lies)' and their Paris For Canal show, recorded that week, also eventually found its way onto BBC's Channel Four.

Arcade Fire's quirky relationship with awards ceremonies actually began during this period as they received Grammy nominations for both *Funeral* (Best Alternative Rock Album) and the 'Cold Wind' single (Best Song Written for a Motion Picture) although, in reality, the song had been bouncing around in demo stage for a number of months prior to acceptance onto the show's lucrative soundtrack.

Just to complete this roundup of myriad success, in Halifax – Nova Scotia, not Yorkshire – they carried off the Juno Award for Songwriters of the Year for three songs from *Funeral*, 'Rebellion (Lies)', 'Wake Up' and 'Neighborhood 3 (Power Out)' and in England they were nominated for three Brit Awards – Best International Band, Best International Breakthrough Group and Best International Album, although they failed to win any of them. Arguably of more importance was a terrific showing on *Later With Jools Holland* where 'Power Out' and 'Rebellion (Lies)' managed to push them through to the second-wave rock audience that, frankly, uses Jools' massively influential programme as their only window into the contemporary music scene. The two performances would later filter onto the Jools collection DVDs. Although the band didn't quite realise it at the time, those two studio performances completely sealed their star status in the UK. Once Jools has been conquered, the UK simply opens up for any band ready and willing to take full advantage.

In his hugely read online 'journal' – he wisely dislikes the ugliness of the word 'blog' – David Byrne wrote: "Saw Arcade Fire at Judson Church where they played for a few nights – they were introducing new material. They got slammed for sound issues in the press as I did recently, so at least it wasn't just me who was getting the sonic criticism. Up in the VIP balcony the sound did indeed suck, so I wormed my way to within a few yards of the stage, in front of one of the PA speakers, and it was wonderful. The new songs are grand, personal, apocalyptic and totally heartfelt. Just to see and hear a band that is so obviously playing from the heart and not making career moves was incredibly moving – but of course the songs and arrangements are good, too. Yes, I could hear little bits of Talking Heads in their earlier material and shows – which was flattering – but now I think most of their influences are pretty invisible. They've become what they are."

Perceptive indeed. Byrne could be forgiven for noticing the Talking Heads echoes of *Funeral* and, in particular, the funked up live versions of 'Wake Up' and 'Rebellion (Lies)', both now stalwarts of their set, that cleverly referenced elements of Talking Heads circa *Remain In Light*. That 1980 album had arrived at the close of post-punk, effectively pushing towards a new phase of world music enlightenment. It was also an album, and perhaps more than any other Talking Heads records, that remained indelibly stamped on Win Butler's heart. For *Remain In Light* was all about breaking down the musical barriers that existed – many had been constructed by the regressive nature of punk – and embracing a wider scope of influence. One of the fears of *Funeral* had been the creation of that 'sound' that, although a rallying call, also intimated the danger of a band closing themselves in. The new material scattered thinly in the Arcade Fire sets of 2005 might not have been heartily received in all areas, but it certainly showed a desire for the band to remain musically transient, lest the second album become a mere evocation of the first. Talking Heads, perhaps more than any other band of the punk and post-punk era, managed to successfully skim their way into different areas – funk, soul, jazz, world beats – that carried them across the divide and into a successful period of enlightened experimentation in the eighties.

Perhaps it was a growing affinity with Irish culture. Perhaps it was simply the right show at the right time, when, during the course of one hour, a band finally shifts from being an emergent promising act to one at the very top of its game. But Arcade Fire's appearance at The Electric Picnic on September 3, 2005, will forever shine brilliantly. Given the use of a Tardis and freedom to roam at will, one could think of worse places and times to land than in the tranquil, wooded arena of Stradbally Hall, Co Laois, just moments before Arcade Fire hit the stage and provided an hour of relentless fervour that will remain fondly in the memories of all who attended, and not least the band themselves.

Speaking to the *Irish Times* on the band's return to the festival in September 2011, Jeremy Gara noted: "It was special, and that's really the reason we're coming back. I don't know what happened when we played, but it was just one of those magical shows that locked in perfectly. The crowd was just totally up for it. It was definitely one of the biggest audiences we'd ever played for at that point, and we played pretty well. It was just a totally magical experience. Ever since then, it's always come up, like, 'Do we play Electric Picnic again?', and either the timing's been bad or we tried doing Oxegen instead – which was also a great experience, but a completely different atmosphere. But, you know, we're really exploratory, so it was great for us to experience both. So we're super, super up for coming back to play it. We actually kind of mapped the whole end of our touring cycle around it – we play that show, then we play Austin City Limits and a show in Montreal, and then we're pretty much done until we have some more music."

Despite Gara's apparent fondness for the Oxegen gig in 2010 – where they nervously followed a set by Jay Z and performed a strangely muted show before a crowd seemingly lost to their charms – it will always be The Electric Picnic that causes grown men to sigh and begin to mumble comparisons with The Sex Pistols at Manchester Lesser Free Trade Hall (believe me, quite the antithesis of an Arcade Fire show) or Bob Dylan's 'Judas' gig in the main hall of the very same building. That may seem to some like overplaying the importance of the show, but something very special happened in that field on that day.

Win Butler: "When we came off that stage I knew that nothing would ever be the same again. I felt that we had reached a level… something that we had always been striving for. We were all of a sudden, a 'big' band, capable of big shows. You could just feel the confidence oozing from every band member."

The set list that day was, in effect, perfectly standard, with no celebrity-aided unexpected twists thrown in. That stated, it must stand as the complete set that carried the band to the first major yardstick moment of their career. 'Wake Up', 'Neighborhood 2 (Laika)', 'No Cars Go', 'Crown Of Love', 'Haiti', 'Headlights Look Like Diamonds', 'Une Année Sans Lumiere', 'Neighborhood 1 (Tunnels)', 'Neighborhood 3 (Power Out)' and 'Rebellion (Lies)'.

It is hard to find a weak moment in such a set. However, even the most perfectly rounded set list can seem jaded on occasion, especially towards the end of a long tour. But, perhaps only once or twice in a band's career, something truly magical happens and all the elements seem to combine to create a set that truly rises above all the others. That this should happen in Ireland is perhaps no accident, for the suggestion that Irish roots stretch into the heart of Arcade Fire is not without foundation. Given the scope and spread of their instrumentation, their distinctive sound does contain a flavour of the large Irish bands who toured the country in pre-war years performing music that echoed down through The Chieftains, Dubliners and Van Morrison. Whether by accident or not, Arcade Fire certainly seem to have tapped into this rich and oft-neglected vein.

The bombastic appearance at Electric Picnic, 2005, certainly adds credence to that theory. Richard Reed Parry, speaking to John Balfe, noted: "It was amazing. It was maybe our best festival show ever. It was off the hook in terms of people singing and being stoked. It was just this incredible, insane feeling. Ireland always is so kind to us. We love playing there. Irish crowds are some of the best in the whole world and Irish people are some of the best in the whole world.

"It's been pretty step-by-step, I would say, as a band. You really just adapt to whatever gets thrown at you, you have no choice really. You can either refuse to adapt to it or adapt to it. I think we've adapted to it with as much naturalism as we could, given the insane circumstances and all the weird, complex, chance factors involved.

"When we first started playing big arenas it was not a great experience, so we figured out what was not good about that and what we could do to improve that. At this point we can have really good shows in huge sports arenas and have it not feel like a big, empty and lonely hall. We've managed to create a sense of togetherness with audiences that can actually still be a fun, intimate – I mean intimate in quotes – experience. It feels like you're in a room with people, not just standing in this vast black hole.

"But to get back to the memories of Ireland. That particular festival meant so much to all of us. It might seem a bit of a cliché, for a Canadian or American band to feel such empathy with Ireland but it is a wholly cultural link. All the members of this band have performed Irish music and Irish-influenced music at some time or other. We have all, as far as I know, spent time reading Irish literature. So it just felt natural to us and we can't wait to get back there."

The continuing link between Arcade Fire and U2 was further enhanced by a joint performance – on several stages – of Joy Division's hugely adored 'Love Will Tear Us Apart'. If one song seemed to epitomise the early fire of U2 – Bono called it "the song with the holy voice of Ian Curtis" – its combination of simplicity and majesty seems peculiarly indicative of Arcade Fire.

The song was always at odds with the remainder of Joy Division's small body of work. Forests of pretentious prose now darken its corners, never failing to miss the glaring irony – that it is a song of release; a cry for freedom that offered just a glimpse of a new life for its writer. Although it carries a sadness for the life he would no longer lead, it boasts a steely and determined lyric written by someone who had already turned the corner, who had, in the crass vernacular of those who seek to steer someone to comfort following a break-up, 'moved on'. It can be a hurtful song, particularly to the individuals involved – and in that I include the other three members of Joy Division. And, of course, there came the final, crushing irony, that it would become the one song that would ease the financial burdens of the band for decades to come.

But the point remains. 'Love Will Tear Us Apart' sees the way forward. Ian Curtis had departed, not from life, but from a way of life. That this release would be cut so tragically short only heightens the irony.

That Bono wouldn't catch that true heart of the song was, perhaps, not surprising. I mean no disrespect and, in truth, Bono's debt to Ian Curtis has never been disputed, least of all by the U2 singer. As such, I have no doubt that his appearance at the mic for this clunky run-through with Arcade Fire was probably instigated for the correct reasons, although cynics may note a desire for him to become linked with the fastest-rising band on the planet.

As for Arcade Fire. If they have a weakness, then it is surely their often rather blasé approach to cover versions. Even when they are virtually busking, as has been the case with them and this very song before, they tend to shy away from instilling the core rhythm with any true sense of individualism. It remains imitation rather than emulation, which is again ironic given Arcade Fire's natural thirst for innovation.

As for this unfortunate and stilted performance, it is safe to assume that the sheer reverence in which they hold Joy Division might account for the lack of adventure. "I think there is something in that," Win Butler admitted when I broached the subject. "It is probably a fair criticism. After all, we have been in awe of that music since we began... well, forever really. It's gold to us. Perfection."

It is perhaps impossible, therefore, to cover such a song in any way other than artless adoration. Nevertheless, I have little doubt that Ian Curtis would have loved the scope, intelligence and adventure of this band. It might be noted that, on a recent trip to Belgium, this writer noticed that Annik Honoré, perhaps Ian Curtis' true muse, admitted to a healthy addiction to Arcade Fire, even to the extent of choosing *The Suburbs* as the soundtrack for our drive into the heart of Holland. When I mentioned this to Will and Régine, they seemed genuinely awestruck,

For the sake of argument, I suggest we all be very sensible and regard the run-in with U2 as mere indulgence and irrelevant to the band's body of music.

The ties with David Byrne, however, were strengthened on February 2, 2005, when Arcade Fire's set at Irving Plaza, New York, included a sprightly version of the beloved Talking Heads classic 'This Must Be The Place (Naïve Melody)' from 1983's *Speaking In Tongues*. They performed the song on numerous occasions, each one taking its respective position on YouTube, and to considerable extremes of debate ("This version just proves how inadequate they are" to "This is so beautiful it makes the hairs stand up" etc). At first glance, it merely cements the relationship between Arcade Fire and Talking Heads, in a musical as well as personal sense, and this is given considerable gravitas by the appearance of David Byrne on vocals. There is little doubt that Arcade Fire had reached a point where their distinctive sound could be readily employed on cover versions and, indeed, that they had grown capable of extending even the most hallowed of songs. Byrne's vocals, naturally, aided the transition here. As ever, they are edgy, neurotic and oddly placed, endowing a simple melody with psychotic levels of persuasion.

Other versions – without Byrne (at Le Nouveau Casino, Paris, France) – see the band stripping the song down to basics, with Régine play-acting and holding the rhythm on soprano steel pan, allowing Win the space to expand the vocals above an uncluttered backing. This version sees Sarah Neufeld's violin take over that edginess – where Win is warm and inviting, the violin pulls the song to the fringe. It is weirdly reminiscent of The Velvet Underground's celebrated tendency to add darkness to the prettiest of tunes; indeed, the prettier the darker, in many respects. This lovely version – in my opinion, although fans clearly disagree with me – projects a Sunday afternoon ambience on a song that had never been in that area before. As it breaks to a close, the violin softens. Most striking, though, and adding to the random nature of a good cover version, is Win's apparently unfortunate mixing up of the words during the intro. This is forgivable and even adds to its charm, however, as his sardonic smile appears to testify. Again, a few fans would leap on this, even asking, "Was he on drugs?" I disagree, choosing to recall the shard of naiveté that often added a spark, rather than detracted from, say, the random live performances of Joy Division. In more recent years, one could see The Editors perform with far greater musicality... and to far lesser effect. It is that naïve element that so enlivens this unusual take on a familiar song.

Arcade Fire's steep and glorious ascent to the top of the festival circuit, in Europe and in North America, might not, in retrospect, seem particularly surprising. After all, all the required skills were firmly in evidence, and if you wanted to construct the perfect festival act, with an all-encompassing sound instantly recognisable from three fields away, and add a live performance of bombastic intensity, full of drama and spectacle, and a string of songs with soaring anthemic choruses, heartfelt lyrics and pounding rhythmic back-beat and finally acknowledge musical history within that sound, encouraging familiarity across the ages and genres, then look no further than Arcade Fire. This certainly isn't a band that some lonesome troubadour might wish to follow on stage.

Despite all this and despite unfolding acres of music press and broadsheet articles, Arcade Fire's prominence at the head of the festival circuit came as some surprise in 2007.

Nowhere was this more intriguing than at Latitude, in Suffolk. It was the one festival, more than any other, that had gained a reputation for overt adult trendification. In short, if you were, say, a mid-forties male, your shaven head tweaked up to date by wearing thick-rim glasses, three-quarter length trousers, a vegetarian diet and a liking for Arsenal, Nick Hornby books, Gil Scott-Heron, Radiohead and Wilco.

Forgive me, I generalise appallingly. For it is no bad thing, and no fault of Arcade Fire, that they had already become "the band to chat knowingly about during the dope-smoking conclusion to a dinner party in Camden Town". Indeed, they had been firmly grasped by an audience old enough to have vinyl copies of Wishbone Ash albums packed away in their lofts.

Latitude, more than any other British festival, catered firmly for the eclectic tastes of British professional middle-class adults. Set in stunning parklands close to the luvvee haven of Southwold, it seemed nothing less than quintessentially English, the surrounding lanes dotted with pink, yellow and blue cottages complete with hollyhocks and disdainful cats. The festival's quirky nod to the Woodstock generation was completed by the act of spraying the resident sheep in psychedelic colours. Hence, you no longer needed to actually take drugs – it just seemed as though you had.

The 2007 bill was also neatly eccentric, as the three major festival headliners certainly testified. On the first night, a rumbling mixture of poetry, comedy and bands such as The Hold Steady, Cherry Ghost and Puressence would conclude with the Damon Albarn/Paul Simonon/Simon Tong/Tony Allen project, The Good, The Bad & The Queen.

This worthy collective indeed had produced a superb atmospheric album, but as festival bill-toppers they were a strange choice, especially given the sullen and wintry ambience of their record. Day two was similarly strange, headlined by the exceptional Wilco, now firmly rooted in their unique post-*Yankee Hotel Foxtrot* period, with homely slabs of Americana spliced violently with invading shards of Krautrock. For sheer adventurism alone, Wilco had been dubbed 'The American Radiohead' and lavish cover features in fringe organs such as *Wire* certainly helped enforce that. And so to the final act on the final day. Obviously the most coveted spot of the festival and, in a festival of this size, surely a legendary name would not go amiss?

But Arcade Fire? Despite their rapid ascent and fevered fanbase, it seemed difficult to comprehend why they had been chosen as the climactic attraction of a top three-day, multi-genre festival.

My one and, despite promises during the writing of this book, only meeting with Arcade Fire came about quite by accident. It came to pass that I was sitting in a lonely shell, backstage at Latitude Festival, awaiting an interview with a British rock star from Sheffield, waiting and waiting, feeling shockingly conspicuous as the area around me was all but cleared. I had started to wonder how I managed to screw this one up. Was I late? Was I early? Had the rock star been delayed in time-honoured rock star fashion? Was he, at that moment, lost or lusting with some soon to be defrocked girl in some parked Winnebago or had he escaped back to the safety of Notting Hill, or wherever bloody rock stars lived these days?

I found myself cradling a second glass of red and fidgeting wildly while busy crew-type people bustled around me, their faces stern in that ominous look of backstage rock-biz arrogance that I had encountered on so many occasions; pushing things around, ushering people hither and thither, talking earnestly on mobiles.

Pondering their familiar and misplaced self-importance, I failed to notice or at least pay much attention to a group of people who had gathered around my table, bringing with them a new energy and a bundle of nervous camaraderie. Indeed, the nerves were palpable, One of them, a petite and entrancing girl, started to dance and whirl. Two more girls ran into the pack, all huddled and lost in their insular quest. Until, that is, the one they called Will asked me questions.

"Where are we?"

"Where are we, huh?"

Only then did I realise that he wasn't referring to the backstage area at all. It was a broader question than that.

"Urgh. Suffolk. East Anglia. Are you Arcade Fire?"

"Yes. What is it with this place? What's the deal?"

"What, with Suffolk?"

"Yeah. Is it a holiday place?"

Yeah. Pretty villages. Coastal resorts. Beer."

"Beer?"

"Adnams. From Southwold, down the road. You should try it. Lovely stuff."

He looked at me with an expression that wavered between curiosity and sheer pity. Indeed, I had expected him to mutter something like, "Awe, you Limeys."

He didn't though.

"You with a band?" he asked.

"No. I am a writer."

Two minutes later, Régine and Win had settled next to Will. Both eyed me with equal curiosity.

"You writing about us?" asked Will.

"No," I replied, truthfully. Well, I wasn't, then. I was supposed to be doing something for *Uncut*, but not on Arcade Fire, whom I so clearly knew so little about. This wasn't going at all well.

"You live around here?" That was Will. Régine was still casting a suspicious eye.

"No. I am from Manchester."

That did it. That ignited the three of them.

"Manchester. Cool place maan. Smiths? New Order? Stone Roses?"

"That's the place."

"You know them?"

"Well... er... yeah."

"What are your favourites?" (That was Régine.)

"You interviewing me?"

"Well, you don't seem to be interested in interviewing us. Hey man… that's more than OK with us. Makes a change. What about Manchester then? Tell us what is it about Manchester?"

"Well it is industrial… has a heart like a village. World's first industrial city. Lots of attitude. Irish heritage… football and lots of music."

"What's your favourite band?"

Bit of a naff question.

"The Fall, I guess."

"You see, I knew you were cool. Maan, The Fall."

That was Win.

"You know them?"

"Totally Wired, maan."

"Yeah, that's them."

These rather bland but intriguing-in-their-own-way questions were abruptly concluded, largely due to the urgent attention of one of those permanently frowning rock-biz people. Casting an unfriendly eye in my direction, he hurried the band into the adjacent camper.

Shrugging helplessly, I sauntered alone from the backstage area and slipped through into the arena where, little over one hour later, Arcade Fire would burst precociously onto the stage.

Of course, my interest was now duly aroused. Having missed the band's Manchester Apollo show earlier in the year, and suffering considerable chastisement from a variety of 'young people' for having done so, I now witnessed Arcade Fire at Latitude.

Nobody tumbles onto a stage like Arcade Fire. Before they did, standing in the backstage shadows, they seemed locked in fraught trepidation. Win Butler's facial features crossed and uncrossed as he slowly nodded his head to some inner rhythm, while behind him stood the rest of them, spinning around in sheer glee, so glad to be here, topping a bill in this beautiful location, with shards of sunlight splicing through the trees and onto a crowd now so vast, like the scene at the last hole of a big Open golf tournament where their energy is no longer dispersed among the many holes, the many bands, but is now wholly focused, thrilling and climactic. Strangely, this band that was about to surge into the limelight reminded me of some amateur dramatic troupe in some lost parochial outpost; despite the cosmopolitan vibrancy of Montreal, Arcade Fire really do seem like party-hopping parochials, lost to their own bonhomie. But, of course, that is the strength. The parameter walls surrounded them, pushing fans, journalists and music industry doyens clean away from their heady, intensive circle.

Soon enough, however, the nerves are cast aside like so many cloaks and, tumbling together in Keystone Kops collective, they burst onto the stage in an explosion of light and fire.

Around the arena the crowd noticeably tightened. Men well into their forties dressed in three-quarter-length canvas trousers and lime green T-shirts screamed like gig debutantes, threw their hands in the air and unleashed cries of delight, cries of glee that carried them back to that first time they caught The Who, or The Clash, or Oasis, depending on their actual age range.

And then came the sound, flooding the arena like some thick, gooey liquid; wailing violins at the edge, throbbing bass at the heart, the ferocious percussion, clipping the ears, hurting a little, and then came a bang. Arcade Fire on stage and beneath the stars, thrilling and spilling over the edge of the stage, each personality – now well-known to this adoring crowd – playing an active role, with Win and Régine swapping the lead, and then Régine moving from the rear to the front, holding the unfolding rhythm in her hand as if it is a tangible object to be catapulted into the crowd, spinning with glee and climbing back behind the drums. To the unaccustomed eye, there is perhaps a touch of affectation in her actions but, of course, Régine had been physically holding and unleashing songs and sounds in this way long before the emergence of Arcade Fire, and long before there was a crowd to watch her do so.

The performance seemed symbolic and, in Britain at least, indicated that Arcade Fire had arrived at the very pinnacle of the live music arena. No one doubted that, and despite the myriad attractions of this particular festival, the band was clearly leagues ahead of anyone else on the bill, as was reflected in the stronger-than-ever ticket sales for Latitude that year. However, such rapid promotion is not without certain problems.

In Britain, elevation to the rarefied atmosphere of a top festival almost always arrives with the cold slap of critical backlash, closely followed by a gradual demonising of the individuals in the eyes of the public. For evidence of this, look to U2, Coldplay and Snow Patrol. Record company pressure, more often than not, sees such acts softening their sound in an attempt to secure and maintain high-level radio play, a situation that echoes back through rock history. While older fans of these bands may feel aggrieved and drift towards smaller, younger, more distinctive acts, there is no doubt that the mass global audience that awaits is unlikely to appreciate too much experimentalism, and while the softening of material is certainly understandable, it's also rather sad when it happens.

With Arcade Fire, however, there is one noticeable difference. They are from Canada and this alone changes everything. Indeed, they had become an integral part of something called 'The CanRock renaissance', which brings both relief and responsibility and needs a little explaining.

There can be no doubt that, despite the disparate backgrounds of the individual members of the band, Arcade Fire became known throughout the world as a Canadian rock band and, within that vast country, as a Montreal rock band. As such they took on board a certain individuality that, quite literally, seems to go with the territory. For instance, there is no real battle between indie and majors in Canada. If you are from Canada, you are pretty much independent of the rest of the world and, for an awful long time, the term Canrock was used in a rather derogatory manner to differentiate music produced by Canadian artists from that of their American counterparts. Not only was this completely unfair, it was – even to distant eyes – blatantly untrue, as could be seen by the success of Canrock artists of the late sixties such as Leonard Cohen, The Band, Steppenwolf, The Guess Who, Gordon Lightfoot, Joni Mitchell and the man generally regarded as the granddaddy of Canadian rock, Neil Young. How could a country that produced such an abundance of talent – and the massive swell of underground music from that period – still manage to attract disparaging sideswipes? Well, probably because Canada borders the USA, which would never allow its northern neighbour to compete on even terms. Even the above mentioned artists, proud Canadians all, have been accused of making their names not within Canada at all, but in the US and, to a lesser extent, in England.

It is perhaps true to suggest that, between the late seventies until 1985, there was something of a slump in the output and quality of Canadian music. Even Michael Barclay, Ian A.D. Jack & Jason Schneider's gargantuan tome, *Have Not Been The Same*, which charts the Canrock renaissance from 1985 to 1995, admits that liking Canadian music at the start of that period was rather like admitting to a strange affinity for turnips. Mention it in knowing rock circles and you would be confronted with, at best, pitying looks or, at worst, withering contempt. There were exceptions. The extraordinary and enduring success of Rush seems to tower so high over Canadian rock of that period – or any period come to that – that it hardly seems to belong to it at all. With Rush in a separate universe, it was left to bands like Loverboy from Calgary to attempt to make that international breakthrough. While it's not relevant here to delve into the complex problems that hindered progress for the Canadian music industry in the first half of the eighties, the one guiding truth seems to be that nobody really looked towards Canada for musical inspiration.

This changed almost overnight in 1985. You could even claim a hinge moment to be the formation of Toronto's visionary Cowboy Junkies. Although they would latterly sell millions of albums around the world, at their inception they were completely isolated within the cultural borders of Canada. They recorded their first album in a garage, pushed it out and literally took it on the road, gaining fans gig by gig. With no music industry infrastructure and no one really looking towards Canada, it is obvious that the Cowboy Junkies saw this humble trudge as their only means of escape.

By the mid-nineties, however, the perception of Canrock had changed thanks to a number of astonishing artists emerging during that period. Many took a lead from the ongoing muse that was Neil Young who also inspired the entire generation of grunge, perhaps the moment when Canadian music was truly placed on the map. Young's disciples included Men Without Hats, Barenaked Ladies, Bruce Cockburn,

Skydiggers, Skinny Puppy, Daniel Lanois, Martha & The Muffins, K.D.Lang, Sarah McLachlan and Blue Rodeo.

All these performers made certain that Canadian rock music would never again be regarded with disdain. By the time that Arcade Fire emerged, Canada was no longer an underdog, yet even as the country forged successful links around the world, to emerge as a major band from Canada still involved overcoming the burden of its chequered legacy. In this regard Arcade Fire are proudly carrying that mantle into a fresh new era, where they would represent a new truth – that anything is possible, *especially* if you come from Canada. That may be seen as a kind of triumphalism, and so it is, and that is what seems to power out of their every live performance. Furthermore, the breakthrough of Arcade Fire in 2004 served to pull many acts along with them in their wake.

Therein lies the true sea change in Canadian music. Not every band is an Arcade Fire but, in translating their buzz into blockbuster status, they have forever helped to change the landscape and break those old restraints, the old prejudices that held Canrock back for so many years. What Arcade Fire have achieved lies true to the Canadian ethos. In signing with Merge and opting to go with Rough Trade in Europe, they have retained their sense of individuality and Canadian resolve. This has reflected down through the ranks. No other band in recent years had been so fortunate, of course, but they have strived to keep their operations close to home. It was the major label system that eventually cracked the Canrock renaissance. However, whatever happens in the future, it is unlikely to happen again. Canadian rock bands remain wary of global pressures. Neil Young, Arcade Fire and Rush have all managed to scale the very peaks of rock's pantheon. Canada is well and truly on the international map – at long, long last.

Chapter 9

Neon Bible

By the spring of 2007, Arcade Fire's genre-defying style dominated everything that was written about them. The depth, power, scope and feel of *Funeral* had opened ears and minds. Acclaimed by just about everybody, it had become one of the true classic albums of the decade, if not of all time. It was only the unique nature of the music, and its propensity for troubling dyed-in-the-wool minds, that prevented if from becoming a 'landmark rock album'. Quite what kind of album it was caused ripples of consternation in an era when albums were marketed simply by genre, thereby quickly reaching their natural place in the market, be it in the CD racks of dwindling record stores or downloaded onto iPhones via iTunes which automatically decrees in which genre of music an album should be catagorised. While in artistic terms a music form that is unidentifiable can only be seen as refreshing and vital, it is the kind of dilemma that brings a puzzling awkwardness to the marketing selection process.

"It is something we are aware of but could never allow to affect us in any way," Will Butler told Australian magazine *Scream* in 2006. "Not one person in this band is built that way. Songs are written and then they evolve and include the entire band, each member adding to the song. It doesn't always work out. Sometimes there are disagreements but that is not the norm. We have come to a place where each musician feels their way into a song."

The writing of songs by Arcade Fire was an organic process, allowing the basic idea of each song to gather instrumentation along the way. While this allows Arcade Fire the freedom to drift beyond the initial stirrings, it also makes it difficult to establish a clear cut direction. Or is that, too, a perfectly natural process? Régine: "I think we have only a vague idea at the beginning. We write songs all the time and it is not always natural for them to fall in with some general concept that may or may not be the next album."

Nevertheless, a collection of disparate songs does not make a cohesive album. There has to be some thread running through them, even if it's ambiguous. This was especially true in the wake of the immense success of *Funeral*, which was virtually a 'concept' album, albeit one born from the most unlikely of sources. That was problem number one when it came to recording the follow-up – how to find something equally identifiable and something that stayed true to the band's natural songwriting process. The problem was exasperated by the continuous touring that occurred as a direct result of *Funeral's* success. Writing on the road rarely met with success.

Régine: "We do write on the road, though. What is not particularly natural for us, is the social expectations of being on tour. Meeting people backstage, whether they are fans or record company people, is not something that any of us are any good at. It's no disrespect, but I don't really want to sit around talking to endless people who I don't know. We do write and work and talk band situations all the time and basic ideas for songs have often come when we are back in some hotel room. Well, we want to work on it there and then. Not be living in some rock'n'roll circus. Perhaps we make bad rock stars but it's just not what we are about. The songs [for the new album] were in our heads for a long time and, basically, we just wanted to get on with working on them."

Nevertheless the problem remained. Would the band continue in the anthemic nature of the songs on *Funeral* or simply rip up that template, deconstructing the very thing that made it so successful and begin again?

Would there be a new concept? Would the production change? More importantly, would they adopt a softer approach to aim for radio play or mount a defiant revolt, closing ranks and rushing headlong in the same direction as before? Both approaches have been tried time and time again to counter the notion of 'the difficult second album', and both have failed. Arcade Fire would not fail.

Arcade Fire's new album would be called *Neon Bible* and a taster for it arrived in December 2006 with the single 'Intervention', initially released on iTunes. The group's pragmatic determination to use their success in a truly practical way could be said to begin here. Proceeds from the single would go to 'Partners In Health' charity.

A curious fault arrived with the initial release as iTunes briefly also released two segued songs, 'Black Wave' and 'Bad Vibrations'. These were withdrawn but only after many downloads had been purchased, although the full extent of the blunder was probably limited to a few fans cherry-picking new tracks – nothing too damaging.

Of more concern was the unofficial leaking of the album on download in January 2007, two full months prior to the release date, though it didn't seem to harm immediate sales, as the album immediately hit number one in Canada and, intriguingly, number one on the Irish chart, presumably after the success of the Electric Picnic show.

Neon Bible? The name is taken from the debut novel of the American writer John Kennedy Toole who was awarded a posthumous Pulitzer Prize for his work *A Confederacy Of Dunces*. He committed suicide at the age of 32.*

---

* Born December 17, 1937 in New Orleans, Toole enjoyed the backing of several big names in the literary world, but commissioning editors rejected his work during his brief lifetime. Born to a middle-class family in New Orleans, Toole was taught an appreciation of culture by his mother, who was thoroughly involved in his affairs for most of his life but with whom he had an often difficult relationship. With her encouragement, Toole became a stage performer at the age of 10 doing comic impressions and acting. At 16 he wrote his first novel, *The Neon Bible*, which he later dismissed as 'adolescent'. Win Butler had read the book while at high school and openly regarded it as a 'lost classic'. Toole suffered paranoia and depression before his suicide in 1969.

Whereas the themes of *Funeral* were mined from the strands of the family backgrounds of Butler or Chassagne, this time an equally unlikely – and equally unsellable, it might seem – fixation dominated the album. As the title strongly suggests, Butler sought to delve into his religious background, schooling and his continued fascination with religion as a subject for study. Indeed, the manner in which *Neon Bible* songs are delivered sounds as though they are coming from the pulpit rather than an arena stage. His vocal approach is akin to 'sermonising', albeit diluted by a deliciously wicked sense of humour.

At the heart of this humour lie the dour predictions and summaries of a weird old America, where schoolboys run amok in school canteens, where the dark heart of racism still thrives and where paranoia simmers on every street corner, in every bar, school and church, and where those religious ties remain solidly entangled within a society edging ever nearer to a national disaster of gargantuan proportions. Such images of home-based apocalypse might not seem like sure-fire winners in the world of album marketing but, again, this is Arcade Fire we are talking about and within the spectrum of their songwriting, more often than not, the worst is something that lies just over the horizon. This is the music of a country living in fear.

Recording this second album was an elongated process that began with the eventual acquisition of a church. While this might, at first, seem like the action of a band suddenly gifted too much money and success, it was an (almost) unprecedented step along the road to realise a physical manifestation of their sound, if not the individual songs.

The church was purchased in October 2005, with the band moving in to begin work on the interior the following month. It says much for their collective work rate that, after only a two-week clean-up operation, its interior was actually ready to be used to record two pre-album demos by December. It was, as Win stated, merely 'the bare bones', of both the new music and the concept of a church studio. During this initial recording, the band survived by using the makeshift kitchen to boil coffee and soup. As the antiquated heating system croaked and groaned a little too noisily to be used as mere ambience, various band members went scouring the local electricity showrooms in search of heaters and light bulbs; not exactly the stable of superstardom but a situation that might be seen as warmly metaphorical, as if, literally, their church was built of song and the sheer force of their ambition.

During the first six months of 2006, the band divided their time between building the recording studio – itself a notoriously painful and obviously complex process – and building bedrooms in the basement, literally bringing a home to life from a dusty shell. In addition to this, they managed to record half an album and scribble the remainder in notebooks. In the process, the building of the church interior perfectly mirrored the building of the new album. There were even times when half-built songs strangely resembled the rooms in which they had been written, their dark shadowy corners and dusty enclaves providing on-tap inspiration. If a certain section of music would prove difficult, the musician in question could, and often would, drift to a lonely corner or downstairs bedroom to contemplate the piece more effectively. Win, too, would spend many hours sitting alone, writing, grasping inspiration from the gothic shadows. One might also assume, given the physical presence of the church, that the walls, ceilings, floors and polished woodwork would all benefit from having the music soaking in for long periods of time. While this might sound a mite pretentious, there is little doubt that churches and other religious buildings are spectacularly 'affected' by the music taking place inside. This is one of the primary reasons why Arcade Fire chose to purchase the church in the first place, locked as they were into the belief that a living music-filled building of such an age and resonance would add to the power of the recording. While standard recording studios can seem sexy and subterranean, they can have a clinical effect on the music, especially if it has been written within those walls. This church was therefore part of an organic process and not as mysterious as it might first appear.

An odd parallel exists here between the church of Arcade Fire and Pete Waterman's church-come-studio-come-offices that thrived at the end of Manchester's Deansgate during the nineties. One recalls 'in-house' producer Johnny Jay, much responsible for the more eclectic dance edge to the strange Waterman empire, explaining the building had a profound effect on the music recorded in it and "… the way in which people worked." It also, for a short while, housed a rock radio station, something that Arcade Fire have also mooted as a possibility for their acquisition.

In retrospect, all the activity in the build-up to the recording of the second album might seem frenetic. In truth, the band had actually taken some considerable time away from the music, as Win Butler explained: "Even though we hadn't played live for a year or so, we were way better at playing together than we were before. There are certain songs on the record, like 'Antichrist Television Blues', where everything was recorded live off the floor, which wouldn't really have been possible to do on the last record. We did a bunch of location recording, like the pipe organ. We went into this other little church and recorded 'My Body Is A Cage' and 'Intervention', and the beds of those were live. Our goal was to take the core of a weird little live thing and do whatever we wanted with it afterward. The last record, we were playing live a lot while we were recording, so I feel like the arrangements had a lot of time to develop, and we wanted to be able to do that with this record, so we'd work for two weeks, then take two weeks off and just go home and play and think about it, kind of allow the songs to evolve."

The religious elements certainly came together more naturally within the setting, with Butler drawing inspiration both from the building and his schooling.

"I studied scriptural interpretation, which is more about how people get meaning out of texts, looking at stuff in the Old Testament – Muslims, Christians, Jews, different interpretations of the same texts. I think there's some pretty amazing language in the Bible. The thing that's always been interesting to me about religion is that compared to the more modern spirituality, the West Coast pseudo-Buddhist thing that people go for these days, actual Buddhism and Islam have been looking at these philosophical questions, at really hard questions, for a long time. There's a lot of stuff that philosophy doesn't talk about, and in the secular world, a lot of times, people don't talk about these ideas, and that was always really interesting for me. The idea of evil and death and love. There's not really any scientific way to talk about it. Whenever you're talking about meaning, basically... I think a lot of the human experience has to do with trying to understand what things mean, and there's not really any tools to do that unless you're thinking about it in a more spiritual or philosophical realm."

The main difference between *Funeral* and *Neon Bible* is a general drifting away from the anthemic towards the oratorical. This stall is set with the opening 'Black Mirror'. Beginning with a foreboding rumble, the song immediately sets a grimly portentous tone as it grinds through a cyclical mesh of unforgiving guitars. At once you yearn for the comparative 'space' evident on almost every song of *Funeral*. But here we have a driving rockbeat so harsh it even starts to threaten the melodic heart of the song. This is only rescued at the very end by the rising bass that, at least, promises to spill into a more uplifting area.

"I know a time is coming when all words will lose their meaning," chants Butler, somewhat depressingly. In the background can be sensed traces of *Heaven Up Here* period Echo & The Bunnymen, the difference being that Butler appears to be chanting wildly against the formidable onslaught of the howling back-beat. Is he, as an artist, in fear of being swamped by the oncoming rush of a black and terrible future? That might be the conclusion. Why else begin an album with a song that self-ignites long before the female voices weigh in with the chant of 'Black Mirror... Black Mirror...'"

The rumble, at least, is infectious. It opens and closes the track like the slamming of a huge steel door, effectively sealing a spirited if ineffective statement of defiance from a band literally battling their way out of self-imposed restraints. In a sense, it's a pure artistic statement and, if not taken literally, might be said to slam against the raised expectation level of the band's situation. If the fans want blood... here it is. In buckets. Gothic and unforgiving. For better or worse. You are already deeply ingrained within album number two.

The second song, 'Keep The Car Running', perhaps kicks back to the previous album. In fact, if you approach this album in search of the lively dementia that pulsated so effectively in the harsher areas of *Funeral*, then 'Keep The Car Running' satisfies that particular urge. Again, soaring melody is dispensed with in favour of a driving, grinding beat. Naturally so, perhaps, given the song's general theme. It is a song of panic, terror and potential pain. A fevered vocal urging us to, indeed, 'Keep The Car Running' and one has the unnerving sense of being in a vehicle being chased at 90 mph by a much darker and more powerful force. The song thunders on in this fashion and, several times, appears to swerve to avoid large immovable objects. As a metaphor, perhaps it could be used to view the frenetic nature of a band that has found massive and almost instant success, hurling them into a world full of crazies and sycophants. Through this they yearn to return to a firm and wholesome artistic base but, day after day, myriad distractions and pressures pitch in and threaten to swamp their very best aesthetic intentions. That perhaps makes light of Butler's lyrical vision, for pitching into the paranoiac mix here is bad religion – perhaps the true theme of the album – rampant disease, surging war, tyranny and pestilence! My goodness, no wonder the passenger is pushing the driver to the limits. Get us out of here.

By now it has become clear to even the first-time listener that this is an album that will continue to wave that 'end is nigh' placard from first chord to last. Nowhere is the thought of impending doom allowed to escape. This is not without its rewarding moments, however. Particularly evident on 'Keep The Car Running' is the kind of adrenalin rush one probably feels when the end is genuinely imminent.

Three songs in, the title track revives the ironic tradition of placing the power of a title track on the shoulders of one of an album's less forthright moments – as in 'Aladdin Sane' or 'Wish You Were Here'. The album dips to a deliberate dirge, 'Neon Bible' creeping along softly, almost wistfully, as Butler's guiding lyrics are matched by Régine's percussion – hitting a door frame, maybe – and what sounds like 1,000 broody dark violins. It is, at two minutes 16 seconds – and it seems shorter – a mere slip of a song and its slightness is amplified massively by its lofty position as title track. Artists often used a similar tactic back in the days of early to mid-prog, wherein an album title pointed towards some irrelevant curiosity, mid-placed on side two, as if to claim that artistic integrity might lie beyond the grasp of the general listener.

As stated, the phrase 'Neon Bible' came from a novel written by teenager John Kennedy Toole, and while it may have been entrenched in juvenilia, Butler never lost sight of certain images. The cover of this album and, indeed, the backdrop of the band's stage set, depicted glowing neon pages being sent out into the ether, in a faintly sinister way, intended to catch hold of gullible ears; maybe a contemporary element of religious mind control. Interestingly enough, when a reader of *Uncut* magazine asked Win Butler if he believed in God, he replied: "Well I don't know. I'm more interested in the questions than the answers. I started out studying fine art at university and then drifted into philosophy and then found myself drawn to religious studies because pretty much all Western philosophy comes from the Bible ultimately. I think that people were asking pretty heavy questions – about existence, about evil, about the nature of the world, thousands of years ago. I don't know if God exists but I can't criticise people for trying to understand these things. And, let's face it, the Bible is a great novella, with plenty of potent images. It's all of Western philosophy crammed into 900 pages."

The next song, 'Intervention', displays both the struggle to gain new ground in terms of songwriting and musicality and the self-imposed confines of the very same. That is the true paradox of *Neon Bible*: three songs in and it has already begun to sound like an album hemmed in by its own adventurousness. 'Intervention' proved nothing if not intriguing. That it continued the quasi-religious imagery is obvious from the second it begins, with Régine Chassagne sitting at a church organ, seemingly fully able to crank the thing into life, feet skimming across the pedals, surly swirl of sounds swilling around the church in which the recording was made. Such an unconventional step was arguably a stroke of genius, firmly establishing the church ambience at the heart of the album and allowing Win Butler licence to bring his vocals down to a level of sermonising. Hence the listener is forced into a pew while the singer gains control, forcing his way into the dominant position while the listener is cowed by the grandiose ecclesiastical finery, accepting all the fire and brimstone without complaint.

Nevertheless, 'Intervention' remains a curiosity. Although technically a dirge, it increases in intensity – in true Arcade Fire tradition – and moves from soft menace to thunderous outpouring within the space of one minute. "The useless seed is sown," chants Butler, which serves only to belittle the listener ever more, albeit with Win's tongue firmly in his cheek,

What transpires is an unexpected step back to the medieval imagery that played a small part in Régine's musical upbringing. If nothing portentous can be made of the lyrics – and 'impending doom' remains the most obvious notion here – then it can be viewed as an open comment on US intervention in, among other places, Iraq and focuses on the human tragedy of such merciless and godless 'intervention'. It is truly mischievous and, with its heart firmly in the right place, we can forgive any element of cod-sermonising. That said, musically it attempts to rival the anthemic peaks of *Funeral*, though is prevented from doing so by its own musical limitations.

On 'Black Wave'/'Bad Vibrations' Régine takes the lead in the first half of – again – a song that splits violently at the halfway stage. What follows is an update and sister piece to the mighty 'Haiti' which, like that song, can be viewed as both a direct comment on the continuing troubles of that intriguing country or, if one wishes, expanded to comment on any country attempting to deal with and recover from a deadly regime. There is, however, hope conveyed by her voice, which, given its multi-layered production, attains the serenity of a church choir. The power of flickering candles, dark corners, polished wood and brasses and the full depth of an intellectual and feminine approach bring light and sympathy to such an appalling scene. In particular, there's a vague reference to guerrilla-held land in Haiti, apparently reconciled in the wake of the disastrous regime.

By contrast, the second half of the song is a wholly masculine affair – a crashing, squealing mess of nature's natural and rampant violence. The song now seems to be about the tsunami of 2004. In stark contrast to 'Black Wave', 'Bad Vibrations' sends shards of pure helplessness in the immediate aftermath of the thunderous crack ('Bad Vibrations'! Don't mean to seem flippant, but what a brilliant title, somewhat lost here in its role as a 'part two'). Quite why the man–made and natural disasters are forced together within four minutes of song escapes me, though both can be viewed as one part of the general breakdown of mankind, weather and the world.

If *Neon Bible* has, thus far, concerned itself wholly with the gargantuan issues faced by mankind, then 'Ocean Of Noise', in defiance of its title, seems to pull back to the dark personal history of Win Butler, perhaps retreating to a lost bedroom in Montreal and a romance that swayed from glorious to something approaching violence. Given its delicious blues-lilt, restrained vocals and – yet again – its gathering intensity, 'Ocean Of Noise' provides one of the true highlights of *Neon Bible*. It is reminiscent of David Byrne and his talent for building edginess and paranoia into small-scape lyrical visions. Here, just two people lie in bed, seemingly at ease yet absorbed by a massive swirl of emotion and regret. Out of the small pops the big emotion and, again a paradox, this small-time story seems suddenly to gain massive proportions as the violins rise and the intensity increases.

Although it would not become one of the better-known songs on Neon Bible, 'Ocean Of Noise' appears to be the glue that pulls these weird and post-apocalyptic songs together. It's also kind of misty in a dank woods and shunting through fallen leaves kind of way; not exactly psychedelic folk but pointing towards that unlikely direction.

The mystical realms of a metaphorical suicide are touched on during 'The Well And The Lighthouse' which sees the narrator driven to his death by falling for his desire and his fear. In the background, there's the ironic chastisement of the devilish muse. This might not sit with every interpretation of this relentless, driven song that, in terms of sheer pounding R&B, might sit well in a Status Quo set if, indeed, the Quo were ever concerned with such weighty matters as grand romantic gestures and eerie surreal dreamscapes.

Despite the constant sermonising and ecclesiastical ambience, the Christian figures who haunt *Neon Bible* are often dragged out in the cold and subjected to a mockery that almost defies Butler's respect for the original Biblical 'searchings' for some kind of truth. 'Building Downtown' ('Anti Christ Television Blues') trips into novelistic tone as it depicts a God-fearing father who, in a courageous though rather foolish attempt to escape the televised horrors of 9/11, hurtles his daughter into the shallow 'glamour' of downbeat showbiz.

Intriguingly, given the New York nature of the song, 'Building

Downtown' contains many echoes of Bruce Springsteen and Butler's voice gathers some of the heartfelt urbanisms of 'The Boss'. It's a speedy little thing, as if hurtling in a rampant yellow cab in 'fast-mo', skimming through the grid system, avoiding the stares of startled pedestrians and annoyed cops with ugly faces.

A song born from frenetic post-9/11 paranoia, its rather warped vision – that God will send him a little girl who will sing the message – becomes rather lost as the fast-paced lyrics scramble away to little effect. The 'hero', truly disturbed that 'the planes keep crashing always two by two' loses all sense of reason as the song thunders on, leaving him to bizarrely ask the question, "So tell me Lord, am I the Anti-christ?"

It's a mixed up, messed up, shook up world and the frantic flashing colours of day-to-day life in New York serve only to intensify the full paranoiac effect. That the song works to thrilling effect is testament to Butler's increasing power of performance – and it seems to belong to him alone as the normally lush and textured background is reduced here to a mere skip and skiffle. In many ways it is the oddest song in the entire Arcade Fire repertoire, especially as it gathers countryesque notations as it moves briskly on, perhaps also hinting at a 'southern man with southern Christian' values lost amid the crazed tribes of midtown Manhattan.

Win: "I think hope only means anything if it's in something real; otherwise, it's just kind of a dream. A lot of stuff is dark in a way, but unless you're really looking at a situation for what it actually is, it's hard to be hopeful – or meaningless to be hopeful about it unless it's actually based in a real possibility. I just saw this thing on Martin Luther King, and before he gave the 'I have a dream' speech, he gave a lot of speeches that were about a more negative dream – that you had to face your broken dreams. He spoke about that a lot, the broken American Dream, seeing it for what it really is, the positive and negative. Sometimes religious thinkers can take that on in a different way. It's sympathetic to the extent that it's thinking about something that maybe doesn't merit a lot of thought. I find that that aspect of the American dream – the *American Idol* world – actually takes up a huge part of American culture right now. I feel like a lot of people really relate to that way of thinking, so I thought it was worth thinking about for a minute."

'Windowsill' is a song of escape featuring a simple Régine thumping back-beat and the Butlers singing "Don't want to live in my father's house, no more". The escape seems to be from all the expectation heaped upon a young man from, presumably, overbearing parental guidance. Expand this further and the resentment might be said to take on board a larger anti-religious sentiment. The escape seems permanent. He doesn't want to give an "address, don't wanna see what happens next" and he certainly "don't want to fight in a holy war". As such, it is a song of both growing world awareness and the increasingly paranoid state such awareness can bring. Especially as his new world wariness seems to fly directly in the face of everything he has been taught and everything his father holds dear. The realisation is truly shocking and he will not even entertain the idea of being visited.

"Set me free, MTV what have you done to me," he cries, partly at maternal misdirection and partly at the education system that – to his way of thinking – attempted to turn him into a monster.

It's a truly stirring affair, metaphorical or not, and the superlative delivery carries with it all the weird mystique of a David Lynch scene. As with 'Building Downtown', and this is a gathering theme, the heart of the song lies in contemporary panic as the world seems to be spinning out of control and people on both sides of the so-called 'holy war' are thrown into the same conclusion. And maybe, at the end of the day, the simple scramble is for oil, for power, or for the status quo.

On the subject of the MTV reference, Win, on the *Pitchfork* website, noted: "I haven't really watched MTV in a long time, since it kind of stopped relating to music. I feel in a way that it's kind of sold out a generation of kids. It's really powerful to youth culture. I found out a lot of stuff through MTV, and I didn't even have cable, I just saw it at friends' houses. But my culture in junior high was totally influenced by it. The thing that's a little depressing to me are these reality shows, like *Laguna Beach*. I think they're supposed to be kind of tongue-in-cheek, like 'laugh at the rich people' shows. But I think the effect that it actually has is that kids emulate it. I don't think they're necessarily getting the ironic level, it's just 'I want that, too.' It's not that I'm like Tipper Gore, that I want to outlaw stuff. It's just a little sad to watch, because it's so easy for 90 per cent of your brain to be filled with things that have absolutely no meaning. If you don't shake out of it, it's just a sad scene."

It becomes clear, as the album edges towards its climax, that its finer moments cluster towards the end. The myriad beauties of the last three tracks are beautifully countered by the lovely and untrustworthy lightness of touch that is utilised to such thrilling effect in 'No Cars Go', soon to become one of the hinge moments in an Arcade Fire set that is full of snapping hinges.

Complete with eighties-style synths and chants, this achingly simple song of ecstatic escape can also be thematically linked to eco standards such as Joni Mitchell's 'Big Yellow Taxi' and Jethro Tull's 'Locomotive Breath'. But it's more delicate and less obvious than that, its sheer feathery air recalling daft television adverts and the silliness that might simply follow the blackness of the end; that over the edge, arguably lost in the madness, we are deliriously happy regardless. They know a place where no planes, ships, cars or subs go. And it's a happy if slightly la-la land which, in itself, is rather scary although they will not let this effect the sheen of serenity. For me, it bears a strange resemblance to 'I Can't Let Maggie Go' by one-hit-wonders Honeybus which reached number eight in the UK charts in 1968 and whose chorus of "She flies like a bird in the sky" was resurrected in the late seventies to effectively advertise Slimcea bread. That song was universally uplifting but this being Arcade Fire, dark musical edges tend to creep in as a voice, lost to the wilderness, is heard to proclaim, "Don't know where we are going... just GO!"

Well it may be a letdown. After all the fire and blood and dark entanglements and massive themes, the album concludes with a song about the – gasp – trappings of being a star in a star band! How difficult it must be, although, to be fair, Arcade Fire have never made a secret of their ferocious loathing of the expectations of life in a top band. So, perhaps it's only natural and fair to hear them 'kicking off' within the framework of what is effectively a soul song and, arguably, the most heartfelt yet least admirable emotion on an album that has patchy elements at the beginning but gathers momentum and gains in effect, intensity and sense of purpose as it goes along. That it doesn't levelly compare with the peaks of *Funeral* is not really any fault of the band. The fact is, it attempts to stretch to different angles and, though occasionally derailed by sheer weight of ambition, is still destined to become one of the top ten albums of the decade – with *Funeral* lodged at number one.

Reviews of *Neon Bible* were not as mixed as one might have expected. Music journalists, in general, still clung on to the band's holy glow and, despite the lack of love coming in the other direction, seemed to accept the sheer impossibility of Arcade Fire's task. Despite a few murmurs that the 'band were taking themselves too seriously' (Allan Jones, *Uncut*), the general opinion was that, at the very least, *Neon Bible* would provide a decent continuum. More than that, its finer moments would surely expand and illuminate a live set that had already set the world ablaze.

In Britain and America, the situation was similarly upbeat, with the album crashing in at number two on both sides of the Atlantic. While this was rightly hailed as a great success, the reviews that surrounded the release seemed rather more tentative. Gone, for instance, was the universal plaudit orgy, with critics falling over themselves to align with the amazing new band that recorded *Funeral*. Perhaps naturally, the second album encouraged a more measured approach.

In *Uncut*, Allan Jones noted: "There's evidence of the demented perkiness of yore on 'Keep The Car Running', but 'Intervention' fair buckles under the weight of its own self-importance. The lyrics evoke regime change, war, poverty, the tyranny of religion, starvation, all manner of calamitous doings. It's a lexicon of legitimate liberal woe, although what precisely Butler is saying about any of these things apart from reminding us that they sadly exist currently escapes me.

"The morose title track and 'Black Wave/Bad Vibrations' are simply glum, while 'Ocean of Noise' is about as gripping as watching a beard grow until the unexpected appearance of slurred mariachi horns, a moment of incredibly woozy beauty and one of the record's musical highpoints. Mind you, things as a whole get better in a hurry after this and there follows a quartet of songs that find Arcade Fire at their most irresistible… The album bleeds out with the self-pitying 'My Body Is A Cage', apparently a stab at a 21st century spiritual, a gospel lament whose humourless self-regard is an uneasy reminder that while there is much here to admire, at its overblown worst *Neon Bible* is one of those records that takes itself too seriously to be taken seriously. Watch it fly, though."

In *New Music Express* Mark Beaumont was less sceptical: "And as we stand, awestruck, through the agoraphobic sociopathy of 'Windowsill' ("I don't wanna fight in a holy war/I don't want the salesman knocking at my door") and the ecstatic escape anthem 'No Cars Go', waiting for the final wave crash of the dark Armageddon blues of 'My Body Is A Cage' to finish us off; as we stand staring humanity's darknesses (war, cataclysm, hatred and fear) square in the eye, we know we've been brought here by an Important Record. A record with the bleak-yet-redemptive spirit of R.E.M.'s *Automatic For The People* and the musical magnificence of a *Deserter's Songs*. But also a record that – as much as *London Calling* or *What's Going On* – holds a deep, dark, truthful Black Mirror up to our turbulent times. After the funeral, the awakening."

In addition, and in full support, *Trouser Press* writer Jason Reeler believed *Neon Bible* to be, "...among the best indie rock recordings of all time".

While the reviews tended to hold on the superlatives that had embellished *Funeral*, the music press did seem to rally behind the band in its wake. Q magazine unleashed a hearty backslap by calling Arcade Fire "the most exciting act on earth". This accolade wasn't given lightly – Muse were in the running – and indicated the extent to which the band's level of performance had intensified during the three years since *Funeral*. Whether one believed *Neon Bible* to be a worthy successor or not, no one could argue against the fact that the true home for these songs was on stage, where every member of the band seemed capable of adding theatrical touches that fired a new intensity. Even relatively subdued tracks such as 'Windowsill' would be stretched to the limits by sheer force of performance, literally conveying the notion that these are highly personal statements rather than mere sonic experiments and run-throughs.

In this regard, Win Butler claimed that Arcade Fire had "learned a great deal from watching U2". While over in Britain – and, indeed,

Ireland – such a statement might be met with a touch of derision – U2 having seemingly moved rather too far into rock theatricals for the tastes of those on this side of the Atlantic – Butler was referring to the Irish band's unswerving professionalism and steadfast work ethic. There is no doubt, however, that after exposure to U2 Arcade Fire's onstage game had been upped considerably. The benchmark had been witnessed and, if they were going to survive at the very top of rock's touring hierarchy, they would have to fire on all cylinders, night after night after night. This was the challenge that stretched out exhaustingly before them.

At the time of the album's release, *Crash* director Paul Haggis made a personal request for 'Anti-Christ Television Blues' to be used in NBC's *The Black Donnellys* show. After consideration – and it would have been a lucrative move – the band decided not to grant licence for this. An odd decision, to say the least.

As Win explains: "That was actually a tough decision, because that's a pretty good show, compared to most of the crap on TV. We watched the pilot, and for primetime TV, it's actually quite good. The whole conclusion was completely built around 'Anti-Christ Television Blues', and I was like, 'Oh no, you guys are fucked! What are you gonna do now?' Every cut was lyrically tied. The whole premise of the show gets revealed in the last four minutes to the song. We all kind of liked the show, but at the same time, it's still our song, and the song doesn't have anything to do with that. It'd be kind of depressing to have one of my favourite songs of ours be associated with this thing it's completely unrelated to. It's more about the context. This show was like a really good TV version of *Goodfellas*. If it was actually *Goodfellas* and that hadn't come out yet, I might've said yes. If it was the fucking *Godfather*, the best film I've ever seen, of course they could use our song."

Despite the pre-album download of 'Intervention', the first true single from the album became 'Black Mirror' which duly hit number one on CBC Radio 3's R3-30 chart for five consecutive weeks, running from March 22 to April 19, 2007. While this might seem a somewhat obscure victory, it is important to note that no other band had ever spent more than two weeks on the top spot.

Win Butler: "We spent so long on the record, and it's all so meticulous – it's good to be able to do stuff that's really half-assed and off-the-cuff, from a creative standpoint. When we did that YouTube video, we had a rehearsal at my house, and we were going to release the track list, and I had Jeremy [Gara, drummer] do a little montage of some of the songs, and when we heard it, it sounded like one of those *Greatest Hits Of The '70s* compilations."

The band famously performed on *Saturday Night Live* on February 7, 2007. It was expected to be a simple run-through of two songs, 'Intervention' and 'Keep The Car Running', sans the inclusion of Owen Pallett who had temporarily departed to work on his solo project under the name of Final Fantasy. The performance was shunted into the legendary by Win Butler's outburst after one of his acoustic strings broke. Seizing the guitar, Pete Townshend style, he ripped away the rest of the strings before smashing the guitar on the floor.

The guitar was noted for having the inscription, 'Sak vida pa kanpe' written across the body in duct tape. Translated from the Creole, the curious phrase means 'An empty sack cannot stand up'. The belief is that this is in reference to the continuing plight of Régine's native Haiti.

Any reservations about *Neon Bible* were arguably silenced by the album's nomination for the Polaris Music Prize in September 2007. This alone sparked a new row when Arcade Fire, allergic to compilation albums as they are, chose not to be included in the award's preceding compilation album. In the event the winner was Patrick Watson's *Close To Paradise* but as clear favourites yet the only act not to be included on the album, a number of critics voiced the opinion that Arcade Fire may have been snubbed. All that transpired was a conciliatory press release from the band explaining that it had been their choice not to be included and, indeed, there were no hard feelings about the awards at all.

The album was supported by a seemingly endless autumn tour with dates across the USA and Great Britain preceding work in Paris with filmmaker Vincent Moon. The initial shoot was an off-the-cuff video session. For a band that had often been uncomfortable with the very notion of a 'promo video', it provided a glimpse of a new way of working, The visual aspects of the band's music needn't necessarily be constrained by the live show and it was thought that a visionary filmmaker might perhaps help them find a further avenue of artistic expression. This is something that they would heartily pursue in the future. However, the resultant film, *Miroir Noir*, although celebrated with superlative-laden reviews, brought with it a number of problems. No least the issue of who was in control of the project.

Chapter 10

Miroir Noir

Arriving hotly in the wake of *Neon Bible* and intended as a supportive twist into the avant-garde came the controversial *Miroir Noir*, a DVD film that would expand the accepted notion of concert footage, blend in slices of documentary footage with lovely lingering languid shots and add the odd disturbing image. The premise was simple: a concert film like no other for a band with no artistic peers and an extension to the imagery that prevailed on *Neon Bible*.

The film has been overshadowed somewhat by a rather ugly squabble between band and filmmaker Vincent Moon, whose skilful work in support of director Vincent Morisset certainly provided the jittery paranoid atmosphere that prevails throughout. Moon's fallout seemed extraordinary, given the all-round artistic success of a film that gained reviews pretty much spanning the spectrum of critical assessment.

When I contacted Vincent Moon, hoping to gain an explanation, he merely replied that, "The film represents a part of my life that I have moved away from and I have no wish to go back there or add further comment. I wish you all the best."

Nevertheless, Moon did post this open letter comment on a variety of websites: "Regarding Arcade Fire... They're not good people, that's it. And I don't mean the whole band – I mean the leaders of the band and their management. What I hate about the band now is that people call them an indie band and they're not an indie band, they are a mainstream band. Maybe they're on an indie label but that doesn't mean anything. Those guys are just making things on a very big level, a very mainstream way of thinking. The way they deal with their business is really disgusting for me. The way they deal with things is awful. Their management are awful, awful people, and I know what I'm talking about. I have some really terrible stories with them."

And the reply, from Arcade Fire manager Scott Rodger, was as follows:

"Dear Vincent, I'm one of the so called 'not good people'. Can we get the camera equipment you stole from the band returned yet? Perhaps if your drug habit could be contained you may actually be able to complete a film. We should have taken advice from our other friends who worked with you who advised us not to. But we thought it would be great. Unfortunately we were wrong. Your move to 'art films', that wouldn't by any chance be circumstantial as no one is prepared to hire or commission you any more?? Telling the truth. It's not that hard Vincent? Now can we get our equipment back?"

Vincent Moon was upset by the way in which Win Butler had taken control over the filming and editing process, tellingly stating that, "It has been edited by far too many people."

This might be a simple case of ego-clashing and one senses that it wouldn't be worthwhile to linger too long on this negative issue. However, Moon's comments did curiously echo those of The Flaming Lips' main man Wayne Coyne who, in 2009, informed *Rolling Stone*: "Arcade Fire are pompous and they treat people like shit... they have good tunes, but they're pricks, so fuck 'em."

Coyne later stated that he wasn't necessarily talking about the band members, but rather their management.

All of which served to detract from a film that survives as, if not exactly a masterpiece, then certainly a refreshing, vibrant study in lo-fi filmmaking.

It is a pity that the spat should take away the shine of this film and it is especially strange as both Morisset and Moon had previously worked with the band to productive effect. It was Morisset who, immediately prior to commencing production work on *Miroir Noir*, created the 'interactive' video for *Neon Bible*, a playful promo, to say the least, which appeared to understand the band's thirst for attempting to create something unique from what was a staid formula. Only The Beastie Boys had previously succeeded in attempting this and it is no easy feat, as the very point of a promo video is to place the product in the shop window by the easiest format possible. MTV, in particular, is not noted for screening unorthodox or potentially controversial films. It prefers quickfire and quick sell and to buck these prerequisites seems a pointless exercise, not least perhaps because to do so seems like a waste of record company advance money. It is a delicate area although, if traversed successfully, can become a stepping stone for an aspiring full–length filmmaker, as Anton Corbijn would later prove, progressing from Echo & the Bunnymen and U2 promos to taking the helm of the Ian Curtis biopic, *Control*.

Therein, perhaps, lies an artistic battle ground, as a band full of visual ideas such as Arcade Fire might clash with a new director who has other ideas in mind. As Win Butler admitted in *Sound And Vision* magazine: "All our songs we feel are filmic and could be expended to satisfying effect by way of film or video. It is just something that is always in our minds, although we haven't really managed to do it in a satisfactory manner, as yet. *Miroir Noir* was an attempt to satisfy that, and we are fairly happy although there were problems."

Vincent Moon had already shot the band in La Blogoteque, depicting them singing 'Neon Bible' while cramped in an escalator under the banner 'Takeaway Show'. This short, clever and grainy film would not only find its way into *Miroir Noir* but could be seen as the dominant aspect, its instant, live energetic feel flavouring the entire movie.

At least the director, filmmaker and band agreed on one aspect. The film should remain true to the idea of catching the band in the rawness of the moment and no amount of editing or post-production effects should detract from that. It would not only remain defiantly unpolished, but provide the effect that 'scenes' would appear to be completely off-the-wall. Hence we find a shot of Butler and Chassagne performing the hypnotic 'Windowsill' in a lift, with Régine using the window as instrument of percussion in a neat throwback to her inventive days in low-brow music theatre.

The performance shots of the full band contain few surprises. The opening blast of 'Wake Up' seems coldly obvious until the jittery shot carries the viewer into the heart of the audience where, of course, one finds the band. Lovely aspects of gaffer tape being applied to megaphone, before the striking opening chords and general chaotic – if not fevered – chanting push the song to newer levels. I particularly warm to the shot of Sarah Neufeld, lost among the crowd, clutching the violin like a shipwrecked sailor feverishly grasping a splintered plank, summoning all her might to mouth the lyrics.

This powerful performance splinters into hurried backstage shots – probably about as close as the filmmakers could get – and the band powering into 'Black Mirror', with Neufeld stomping away, as if performing in some raging death metal troupe. Its effectiveness is demonstrated as, within two minutes, the link between *Funeral* and *Neon Bible* is – for better or worse – firmly established.

Chapter 11

Heavy Load

The subsequent heavy touring schedule to promote *Neon Bible* did manage to throw up a number of highlights. It began cautiously, with a series of concerts in churches and hand-picked small venues in Ottawa, Montreal, London and New York. This sensible tactic eased the band into a 23-date European trek, the only downside being a nine-date cancellation due to a virus that rifled through the band's ranks. Nevertheless, they continued through the first leg of a large American tour, taking in a further appearance at the Coachella Valley Music and Arts Festival on April 28. This, their second appearance at Coachella, was viewed as their first American festival outing in the position of undoubted bill-toppers.

The same could surely be said of their Glastonbury Festival show on June 22, which duly cemented the band in the unparalleled hallowed place reserved for legendary Glastonbury performances. Win Butler fully understood the gravity of the situation when he told the BBC: "There is nowhere on Earth like this. We feel as though we are playing to the whole of Europe when we are on that Glastonbury stage… There are many great festivals and we are lucky to be able to perform at so many of them. But Glastonbury has a special power. Everybody knows that. And for a band to tap into that power, well, it is a bit humbling, to stare across that crowd. All those people. All those stories. It is a big, big honour for us. All we ever dreamed of. Well, it's more than that."

Ten more North American shows followed, during which they were ably supported by LCD Soundsystem on a tour that saw a powerful friendship develop between the two bands. Dates in New Zealand, Australia and, finally, Japan sealed the immense schedule that lifted *Neon Bible* beyond the scope of its illustrious predecessor.

Nevertheless, the heavy touring schedule was starting to take its toll and, it must be noted, a certain staleness began to creep in. This was hardly surprising after a year in which they performed 122 shows in all, 33 of which were on the festival circuit. The sheer logistics of such a schedule alone would be difficult enough for a standard four-piece rock band, softly shunting from limo to hotel to venue to hotel, However, with a band of seven – with occasional additional musicians – all performing multi-instrumental roles, matters were complicated further, and at every single gig. The mere act of soundchecking, complex enough in the modern arena, is made far more difficult by the use of no small number of unconventional instruments. Even given the services of their regular sound crew, the act of getting the full and near perfect sound to every member of the audience, in either an auditorium or a festival environment, is an exhausting and difficult process at the best of times. Add to this the myriad problems with travelling to and from 75 cities in 19 countries and you have one of the most difficult band schedules in recent years.

Given all this, it would be pretty staggering if the band didn't suffer from a creeping staleness that started to see a few less than enthusiastic reviews in the press and online. However, though talk of splits within the band would seem to be exaggerated, if not largely unfounded, it was perfectly clear that a break was needed. *Neon Bible* had performed well, although it failed to build significantly on the back of *Funeral*. Perhaps more worrying was the often stated notion that it was *Neon Bible* itself that instilled some kind of gentle decline. Time, therefore, to head back towards a near-normal life in Montreal. Batteries were in dire need of a recharge. The band was aware and sufficiently worried about this for

Win Butler to make the announcement in his online blog. There would now be a resting period.

North American rock music and politics, be it in the USA or Canada, have been uneasy bedfellows in recent times. Indeed, to declare a political allegiance, let alone perform free concerts in support of a cause, is often regarded with a degree of suspicion – and for very good reason. Few could argue that Arcade Fire have shied away from expressing political opinions and backing this up with tangible action, as in the case of their constant help with the problems of Haiti. At last, perhaps, here was a band that was prepared to show unselfishness in this respect.

One of the figures that has loomed heavy in the life of Win Butler is Barack Obama. Indeed, it was during the finish of the New Hampshire Primary when Butler declared his political allegiance. It would seem that the rest of the band were similarly enamoured, as Arcade Fire performed two free concerts in support of Obama before the Ohio State Primary on March 2 and 3, 2008. They returned to the cause in Carolina on May 1 and 2, performing a further two free sets with support from their label owners, Superchunk. Taking place in Greensboro, and Carrboro, North Carolina, both concerts generated acres of press attention in the local media and fanned out to national level as well. In addition, Jay Z joined Arcade Fire at the Obama Campaign Staff Ball, both band and rapper attending at the direct request of Obama himself. Not since the legendary rock-orientated Clinton inauguration had such high-level acts seemed so visible on the American campaign circuit. At the gigs, Butler openly thanked Obama for stating his intent to close the controversial prison at Guantanamo Bay.

Win Butler: "I've seen Barack Obama speak a couple of times, and I really like him. There's something going on behind his eyes, and I think he's really intelligent. But part of me just knows it's going to be Giuliani and Hillary Clinton, which really bums me out. But part of me wants to believe that it could be Barack Obama and John McCain, and there'd be an actual debate. The country needs a real debate so badly. A lot of times, politicians try to overwhelm the general public with how complex an issue is. In a way, I think that's why the anti-war movement in the States isn't as big as it should be. People are overwhelmed by the complexity of the situation, but I don't think a 16 year old should have to know how to solve the problems in the Middle East to be like, 'Fuck, we should not be in this war.' But there's this idea that you have to know how to solve the world's problems in order to feel that something is morally wrong. I'm always back and forth between optimism and depression about the situation."

Régine Chassagne has also helped launch an organisation called Kanpe (Haitian Creole for 'to stand up') to co-ordinate NGO responses to the ongoing crisis. "It's emergency after emergency in Haiti," she said, "because the country's infrastructure is so weak, but one of the things we are working on is long-term aid and co-ordinated organisation. It's less immediately rewarding, but so important."

Chapter 12

The Sound Of The Suburbs

After a 'difficult' second album, darkened further by the various difficulties of the *Miroir Noir* film and the subsequent fallout from the Vincent Moon affair, came the most delicately balanced and precariously poised moment of Arcade Fire's history. There had been much talk, much speculation, much backstreet and internet hype around the recordings of *The Suburbs*, with many suggesting a softer approach than the deep tugging and not entirely sellable emotions of *Neon Bible*. More pertinently, suggestions also arrived via the digital ether that certain 'religious elements', whether ironic or deeply ingrained – or both – would be less in evidence, lest the vast mainstream that lay beyond their core audience be deterred from finding Arcade Fire to their liking.

But, of course, with Arcade Fire, nothing is quite so simple. This isn't Buzzcocks circa 1978, and their dilemma over whether to tread further Beefheartian leanings or opt to become a post-punk Herman's Hermits (no put-down intended). In purely aesthetic terms, Arcade Fire are a vast and complex supertanker, complicated further by the machinations of their band dynamic, and further still by the sways and emotions of family elements within that dynamic.

It was a question of steering forward while retaining their celebrated "… outraged, elegiac vitality…", as Paul Morley wrote, and I take his point. The sense of outrage within Arcade Fire aims at the multitudinous absurdities that confront them on a daily basis, many of which are the dense insanities that confront us all. But, with Arcade Fire, no band has evolved into such a huge and sellable commercial beast while carrying with it a pure musicians' sense of outrage at the way music is wrapped and slapped into an 'acceptable' genre and quickly commercialised, while genuinely pure and artistically subversive acts languish in cultish obscurity. This aspect of Arcade Fire's situation is further enforced by the turbulent wake of the credit crunch and the global turmoil within the music industry, all of which set the scene for the group's 'difficult third album'.

On the subject, Paul Morley perceptively noted: "Arcade Fire, being discriminating pop historians, fully appreciate how the third LP is an important turning point, wherein you need to show how you can still be yourselves without repeating yourselves. One of the Arcade seven, Will Butler, sunny brother of dashing group supervisor Win, who is husband to group spirit Régine Chassagne, in a group that unashamedly mixes family love with an evangelical sense of mission and conspiratorial intensity, admitted to me that he was thinking of Björk's third proper album, *Homogenic*, and the third Radiohead album, *OK Computer*, when they were recording their third. Win didn't say as much – I'm just guessing – but I imagine he was thinking of Springsteen's *Born To Run*, The Clash's *London Calling*, The Smiths' *The Queen Is Dead*, Talking Heads' *Fear Of Music*, John Cale's *Paris 1919*, New Order's *Low-Life* and Hüsker Dü's *Zen Arcade*. For Régine, perhaps: Ella Fitzgerald's *Lullabies Of Birdland*, Prince's *Dirty Mind* and Abba's third 'limo' album."

Personally I might add *Led Zeppelin III*, probably the most underrated of all their albums and Elbow's lost *Leaders Of The Free World*, which was cruelly ignored but is quite perfect.

If anything, Arcade Fire would be even more nervous just prior to the release of *The Suburbs* than they were to the – arguably – less accessible *Neon Bible*. However, in the immediate aftermath of release, commercial fears, at least, seemed unfounded. In artistic terms, it would be rather more complicated.

Win Butler: "A few days (before the first-week figures were announced), one industry predictor guy who's very accurate said our album was going to be number two, like 5,000 copies behind Eminem. But the digital guy who works at Merge was like, 'No, it's going to be number one.' He was the prophet because he knew the other predictors weren't counting indie stores. And the indie stores totally came through and pushed us just over the edge. I hope not. [Eminem] did sell like 29 million [copies] of his first album."

The title track would introduce the album and set the tone for its prevailing feel. As such, it is arguably the most important song and recording in Arcade Fire history since, following the comparatively 'difficult' nature of the admittedly underrated *Neon Bible*, the entire future of the band was delicately poised on the release of their third album. What's more, the first song would set the tone for not just the entire album, but lay out any changes in direction. More importantly perhaps, it would determine whether the band was moving further into the darker areas of *Neon Bible*, or pulling back towards a slightly more radio-friendly stance. As such, the band was acutely aware of the need to produce an album that sufficiently reinstated the sense of critical awe that flourished in the wake of *Funeral*.

It's worth noting here that commentators of British broadsheets had already broken from their previously reverential stance and, on numerous occasions, had started to refer to Arcade Fire as "ever so slightly overrated" (*The Times*) and "critically lauded and fading" (*The Guardian*). Part of this backlash could be nothing more than a natural reaction to the relative failure of *Neon Bible* and if so, fair enough. However on a more localised scale – within London media circles, to be precise – it could also be the consequence of being continually highly regarded by a journalist with such a high and controversial profile as Paul Morley in *The Observer*. Morley's somewhat defiantly stylised writing beautifully builds the band into a critical corner, adding huge kudos with *Observer* readers but, at the same time, partly alienating critics who object to his style. This may not initially appear so important, but the ripples of both Morley's prose and the subsequent backlash are instant and global within the digital landscape of 2011.

All of which added further pressure on the group and the new album's signature song. And, here comes the twist. 'The Suburbs' – the song – arrives in almost shockingly softened mode. The lovely, coddled and dipping opening chords lead to a gentle vocal entrance that offers the almost defiantly bland line, "In the suburbs I, I learned to drive..."

Has there ever, in the history of rock music, been such a beautifully delivered anti-climax. From the second those lines first poured from radio speakers, it was clear that *The Suburbs* would be an album that contained all the commercial attack of, say, U2's *The Joshua Tree* or Fleetwood Mac's *Rumours*. Of course, Arcade Fire being Arcade Fire, the lyric which followed and floated on the gentle hillocks of this song, would twist again, from a statement of suburban bliss to that explosion of dark undertone that results in localised warfare between "your part of town and mine".

In the centre of this unlikely suburban action exist a boy and a girl, very much in love and seeking for a way out. While the romance between Win and Régine was a far cry from some straightforward suburban idyll, it's difficult to listen to this song without seeing younger versions of them as the central characters. With this in mind it might be concluded that Win Butler is deliberately fictionalising his own past; carving a more spectacular and dramatic scenario from crushing monotony. From this lyrical viewpoint it seems quite fitting that 'The Suburbs' should be such a gentle stroll of a song; as effortless as walking a dog on a beautiful spring day around clipped precise lawns, neat rows of plants and sparklingly pristine cars. It's all very David Lynch and, of course, at heart blacker than the darkest night and not gentile at all.

Régine: "No, it's not about just Houston, but both Win and I grew up in the suburbs. I grew up in Quebec, he grew up in Houston. What was interesting to me is that even though the places we grew up in were very different there were feelings and emotions attached to our surroundings that transcended the culture. We could both relate to the same sentiments even though we were in different countries. That's why this album has 15 songs. I think it was interesting to describe all those feelings. For example, the feeling when you're very young that suburbs are kind of nice because there's a little park to go to and it's safe, but then you grow up and as a teenager it seems kind of dead and you feel like you want to get out of there. The image of the suburbs is not very glamorous and it's not something people are very passionate about, but there are still dramatic stories that happen there. Everyone has their own little suburb story."

The second track, 'Ready To Start', is a song born of frustration, initially written during Win's art school days. He was certainly comfortable with the possibilities of his own talent, perhaps naively so, but he was also all too eager to set his ambition rolling. As he hinted, he felt detached from the many societies, clubs and general social order of college life, and felt that heady rush of uncontained ambition, a desire to prove to the world that he has something unique to say.

Paranoia runs deep within this song. Refusing to go out drinking with the lads, he accepts their claims that to step into the music industry would see his dreams torn apart by the cut and thrust of business. As he sings: "If the businessmen drink my blood, like the kids at art school said they would, then I guess I will just begin again."

Of course, setting a song within the time zone of his own studenthood might well be delivered with a knowingly retrospective smile. While the song may have been formed 'back then', it was perfected and delivered by a man leading one of the most successful bands in the world. Not that many years had passed, but Arcade Fire's star seemed to have been flying for an eternity and Win could only look back with a wry smile and, perhaps, just a twinge of regret. It lacks the edgy uncertainty of, say, Ian Curtis in a similar position singing: "Got to find my destiny, before it gets to late" but where Curtis was almost admitting that it was already too late, the Win Butler of 'Ready To Start' is comparatively self-assured and at ease with his new life.

Win: "America's a big country. There're still way more people who've never heard of us. For me, the feeling of 'Ready To Start' came from going to art school and meeting a lot of people who had really defined political ideas and rules about art. But I just wanted to make something in the world and worry about the rest of it later and not get too caught up in rules."

Win, this time to Chris Cottingham: "In my experience, it's not a conscious decision [to make an album about the suburbs]. You just get inspired by what you get inspired by. I got a letter from an old friend and it had a picture of him and his daughter at the mall near where my brother and I grew up [in Houston, Texas]. It was unforeseeably moving and it brought back a lot of memories. This combination of someone that I hadn't seen for a long time and his daughter who I'd never met and a totally generic but familiar place. It was this conflicted but very deep feeling. I try not to psychoanalyse myself too much. Montreal is the place I've lived longest besides Texas. I've been there for almost 10 years now. Next year I will have lived in Montreal longer than I've lived anywhere. It feels like home. Even though Houston is currently the place I've lived longest in my life it's the place I feel least connected to, so even though it's not all literal and not all about me, I wanted to make a record about that feeling."

Maybe the third song, 'Modern Man', digs even deeper. You can trace a lyrical line straight back to The Rolling Stones' 'Satisfaction' here, although urban existentialism is where the comparison ends. This simple tale of dissatisfaction in the digital age sees the narrator suggesting that all is nearly right and correct within his dreams but in reality, something is missing and it's difficult to understand how it is to feel human in a world where you are regarded as a number. Nothing new here, of course, and probably one of the more obvious lyrics within their repertoire. However, 'Modern Man' is probably of more interest for the music, which continues the slick production vein of the album while borrowing heavily from the lighter side of The Cure/New Order axis. The fact that it is a guitar that kicks in with that fabulous English melody rather than, in the case of New Order, a bass being played as lead guitar is hardly noticeable. 'Modern Man' could have been plucked straight from the British charts in 1983, with its lovely choppy rhythm so reminiscent of 'Everything's Gone Green', 'Age Of Consent' and 'In Between Days'. There is little darkness to the song and, despite its effortless zeal, it doesn't contain the intrigue of the songs that cluster around it.

The next song, 'Rococo', is rather more difficult to assess, even if it contains echoes of 'Haiti'. The simple act of weaving the lovely if awkward word 'Rococo' into its position as a one-word repetitive chorus might not seem particularly attractive. Nevertheless, the repetition works.

For many, the first time they encountered this song was during the band's set at Glastonbury in 2010, a performance that gained enormous universal penetration as it was broadcast live across the world – and what an odd little song it was to capture such attention. "Rococo, Rococo, Rococo" sang Butler, over and over, the band changing musical gear behind him before an audience both befuddled and enraptured.

Win Butler: "I probably heard about the Rococo period through Régine, who was really into medieval art when she was younger. Not like Renaissance fairs, more like learning ancient languages. And while there are so many beautiful Baroque churches and it's a beautiful artistic tradition, it almost gets hideous and grotesque if you push it further. You can take something beautiful and overdo it.

"I had a similar feeling about the current information age, where you have all this information that you don't need or want but the medium is there so it's filled up. I was trying to think about this very modern idea using the same language. Also, though it's not really in the song and I don't think anyone would ever pick it up, that same period was the most opulent time in French history, and the darkest shit was going on in Haiti at the same time. There are these images of French aristocrats with big collars and big hair in the jungle in Haiti trying to do their tea parties with flies buzzing around. That was a little bit of the feeling behind it, too."

Beginning with a massive, earth-shattering chord, 'Empty Room' is one of the strangest 'lonely' records ever recorded, especially as it moves from the narrator sitting in an empty room saying their lover's name in nihilist fashion before the whole song opens up like a full-on cathedral choir. This lifts the track to almost spiritual proportions. The production here, it needs to be said, is probably the most fantastic on the three albums, moving from the train-like chug of the opening chords to a state of ecstasy. 'Empty Room' may be a short song (only 2' 51"), but never does it feel small. Indeed it is quite the opposite. And if the band had been tempted to open it up and stretch it over six, seven or eight minutes – and surely they were tempted – then it would somehow have lost its sense of grandeur, rather than gained more. As it is it ends like a train crash and segues thrillingly into 'City With No Children', an altogether different proposition.

Memories. Driving beat. Lost love in Houston. 'City With No Children' begins with the great line, "The summer that I broke my arm, I waited for your letter." It is all in there, really; a year-long first love, unrequited and faded to dust. This is a song that literally drives straight to the heart of the suburbs… of adolescent memories and powerful waves of first love. The problem with a love that dies, even if it's just teenage lust and crush, is the loss of the possibility of a life that might have been lived with that person, fanning out through children and holidays and the life shared. This complete life might be lost over a stupid argument or, in this case, an expected letter of sympathy that never arrives. Here you are, nursing a broken arm while the girl you believe you love is living another life, with someone else, maybe even unaware of your plight. It is a juvenile pain revisited and is far from easy to bear because of that. The city with no children is a life with no love and the reference to the emptiness of the millionaire merely enforces that point.

On 'Half Light 1', Régine steps to the fore with what might seem like her own memories of things past. It seems like an accusing song. While strings swirl to evocative effect, the older girl – Régine – casts a thought back to the loss of that first love. Unlike 'City With No Children' this carries no true sentiment, indeed, and while the backing crashes like storm waves on the rocks, the female voice seems distant, aloof, superior even, as if safe in the knowledge that, back then, she made the right decision and life is better now; much better in fact. If this seems like arrogance from beyond superstardom, so be it. Dipping back to touch an old life – presumably real – is an effective and ancient trick, once perfected by Van Morrison, notably in 'Brown Eyed Girl' but also in various personal references that pepper his songwriting and continue to do so. It works on two levels – alerting old emotions in the old hometown while providing a platform for the artist. 'Half Light 1' is a squint through the mists of time. Not unhappy, not sad, just coldly reflective and thoroughly sold to the spirit of moving on. Sometimes, to move on, you have to look back. This entire album is captured by that spirit.

By contrast, 'Half Light 2 (No Celebrations)' is a non-emotional acceptance of changing times, falling markets, failing systems and the very real notion that the world as we know it is never going to be the same again. I admit, I do not understand the 'No Celebration' add-on to the title. Not that this sounds remotely celebratory. The story is of a move away from San Francisco – although it could be anywhere – and a move east, although the move could also be anywhere.

"Though we knew this day would come still it took us by surprise," sings Win, as his life moves one step further from the memories of childhood. There is also an eco section, stating "Pray to God I won't live to see the death of everything that's wild".

The backtrack to God seems to be a climbdown from anti-Christian mode perhaps or maybe the simple fact that, when all else fails, when science and politics crash, there is nowhere else to turn to other than God. One thinks of Leonard Cohen writing, "I walked into an empty church, there was nowhere else to go."

'Surburban War' is a song that, at the outset, contains hints of Morrissey's 'There Is A Light That Never Goes Out' with the opening salvo, "Let's go for a drive and see the town tonight." But this is a post-suburban war song that even blames the music that divides the youth into tribes. The talk of growing and cutting hair is a reference to the different stages of growing up, but there is still a yearning here as Win states that, "The cities we live in could be distant stars while I search for you in every passing car." This is another Arcade Fire song that changes gear and intensity halfway through and for no logical reason.

Is 'Month Of May' punk rock? Ha! Hard to dislike the ferocious pace here as the voice tells you that "Gonna make a record in the month of May". The Ramones pace never falters either, reminding us of that wonderful release when all music crashed down to a playable simplicity and it felt good to be alive and free once more. 'Month Of May' could really be a reference to the youthful age when one feels full of vigour, life, passion, love, hope and expectation. Listening to 'Month Of May' is rather like digging out that old Stiff Little Fingers album and once more feeling the thrust of wild youth. Thrillingly, it is a song that seems not to really belong on *The Suburbs* but, that said, it is impossible not to fall in love with it and to yearn, once again, to relive life in that ecstatically sexy month of May.

In contrast, 'Wasted Hours (A Life That We Can Live)' is gentle, cinematic and reflective, a lovely celebration of childhood boredom, hour after hour of not knowing where to go and what to do, unaware of the rules, unaware of where ambition and guile may tale you. Yet again, the reference is to "endless suburbs stretched out, thin and dead". That somnolent haze that drifts by on a Tuesday afternoon, broken only by the voices of children in the playground and occasional delivery trucks. In many ways, it is the most simple song on the album and an honest reflection of a time of pre-sexualised wonderment. The nostalgia here carries little sentiment. It is merely a statement of how it was before true life and hope and passion kicked it. The child wonders, 'Is this it?'

And in the next song lies the answer. 'Deep Blue' is the realisation that life really does begin when you find yourself happy in your own skin. It has a curiously icy, synthetic quality. It is intriguing to hear what Win Butler says about the balance between the initial demo, which carried a certain magic, and the moment it became a band song. And yes, there is more than a mere echo of the eighties with, perhaps, the added guile of Radiohead,

Win: "A song like 'Deep Blue' we tried many different ways. We finished it as this total synth song and it kind of left us cold. Me and my brother were playing around with some stuff at home and we found this balance between this almost demo quality and the synth stuff. While making this record I re-read Ed O'Brien's diary about making *Kid A*. There were a couple of songs where he says, 'We started this a year-and-a-half ago and it's the simplest song on the album. We've just mixed it and it sounds like how it did on day one. It took us a year to finish.' I think sometimes the simplest stuff takes the longest. The two 'Half Light' songs we recorded on this tape machine at home. There was something that we really loved about the demo and we were trying to make it a band song and trying to find this balance between what made it exciting in the first place and making it a song for the whole band. In my experience there are certain songs that the first time you play them they are never better and you spend the whole rest of your career trying to get back to the time you first played it. Then there are other songs that you've toured for two years and they sound great. When you try to have both of those kind of songs on a record it's a real juggling act."

In 'We Used To Wait' we find the snap of the snare. More icy synth, could have been pulled from early Depeche Mode, a touch of eighties glare and pulse. Yet again this song talks of the wasted hours of youth, of hanging around, emotionally frozen in the suburbs.

Listening intently to *The Suburbs* brings about the realisation of how few albums in rock history can relate to it. There are wounds and heavy emotional scars in this music, but they lie in subtle, mundane reflections. Compare this to, say, the obvious deep cutting wounds of Dylan's *Blood On The Tracks* where emotional entanglement is like a twining black hell. On *The Suburbs*, the wounds seep rather than gush, like long-lasting open scars, glassy eyes rather than weeping tears. Strangely, it doesn't even relate strongly to *Funeral* or *Neon Bible*, both of which brim with more immediate imagery. Here we are still in the land of dull, old-fashioned furniture, clipped lawns and paving stones. In many respects, 'We Used To Wait' is exactly the same sentiment as 'Wasted Hours'.

Win, to Chris Cottingham: "Music is always reflective of the time in which it was created. It's something that you can hear in music no matter what it's about. To me that's one of the things that's interesting. It's not like making psychedelic music is the most genius idea of all time, but there's something that really dates it to its own time. That's what makes it interesting, not talking about giant mushrooms. This sense of something being in a time." Régine: "After *Neon Bible* we took a year off, just staying at home and writing songs and doing regular things. That was a very happy time. *The Suburbs* reflects that, yes."

Jeremy Gara: "The time off really made a massive difference in terms of feeling creative. We really went into this wanting to do it, which is a positive way to be feeling. When we recorded *Neon Bible* we hadn't taken a break and we had just come off an extended tour for *Funeral* and the world at large felt tense. I think that can't help but have infiltrated

141

the sound of the record a little bit. Also, *Neon Bible* dealt with global anxieties.

"'Sprawl 1 (Flatland)' could be about not wanting to live in the States. And musically it feels like a darker record because it was super ornate with strings and lush, emotional instrumentation. This one, there's still emotion in it, but the subject matter demanded a little less ornamentation. There's not as much orchestral elements on this record. It's replaced with synths and it's a little more percussive and a little more rock'n'roll. One of the reasons it sounds lighter is that the arrangements are not as overblown as they've been in the past because the material didn't demand it."

Naturally, this is followed by 'Sprawl II (Mountains Beyond Mountains)', which completes two songs that could be one. Here are two emotions: one lost in the surburban sprawl and the second, 'Mountains Beyond Montains', sung in a state of exaltation after escaping the trappings of the sprawl. It seems odd, perhaps, to hear Régine's voice on here. One would have thought that after living through the hellish regime of Haiti, a comfortable suburban sprawl would be most welcoming. But 'Sprawl II (Mountains Beyond Mountains)' is a song of joyous escape and true freedom, a reaction to those who ask you to "cut the pretension and punch the clock", a fight to follow the artistic muse no matter how rugged and unrewarding that road might seem. This is the first truly post-success song on any Arcade Fire album and it points significantly to a brighter future where, given the power of stardom, it really does become possible to change things, to influence and inspire. Arcade Fire have reached their state of celebration, at last.

The closing 'The Suburbs (Continued)' could, fittingly, be exit music from a film since it imparts the unworldly feeling you might enjoy when you leave a cinema after seeing a particularly moving film. Part of you is still living in the movie, transported to another world, full of drama and mystique. You can even feel the same way while walking out from a heartless multiplex and this same sensation is true to the heart of this album. It is, after all, an album of drugless, altered states.

Jeremy Gara: "When we were in the middle of recording it late last year I felt awful. It felt like the hardest process of all time. Just because it's more material than we've ever recorded. It became clear how long the record was going to be. It was like, 'Oh my God, this is so much material'. We were working on twice as much material as *Neon Bible* and trying to do it in the same time frame and it felt awful at times. But we always do that. We record until we're sick of the process. The albums are better for it because we've put in all the energy we can muster." Win: "Some of the stuff was the easiest we've ever done and some was the hardest. There are six more songs than on our previous two records, so we were recording a lot more material. This record is really like a double LP: it barely fits on a CD. It was that much more work."

"I think a lot of artists spend their whole career writing about the same ideas. Francis Ford Coppola keeps looking at the same things in every movie he makes. Bruce Springsteen is singing about the same thing in every record he makes. I don't know why that is. I think you're drawn to the subject matter you're drawn to. A lot of times, as you change, you approach it from a different perspective and get different insights. I think that's what we've done here."

Régine: "I don't know. I don't analyse things. It just came out like that. It's not something that you plan. The album is not one judgment on the suburbs. It's more cinematic, like scenes around the suburbs. Do I think it would have been a different album if we'd made it when we were teenagers? Of course, but you could go on and on like that. What if I had blonde hair or lived in Paris?"

"If it stops feeling organic," Chassagne told *Rolling Stone*, "we'll stop doing it. I have no ambition to be the biggest or the bestselling. That kind of thing is not why I, or any of us, play music. There was a time when selling even 10,000 records would have seemed like the greatest, most unimaginable thing in the world but now we're here at this mad point. We're just going with it to see where it leads."

Jeremy Gara: "When I look at a lot of other bands, it does seem that we're the strange minority. We're a disparate bunch but we're similar, too, and we are all friends who respect each other enough not to start jostling for position. It's all very healthy. When it stops being meaningful, we'll have to change. I'm in it for the long haul, though, and so is Régine. This is our life now. It's what we've done since we met. And, it's a good life, a great life. It was such a blessing to really be able to achieve what we wanted to achieve and to be able to pay for it ourselves and do it ourselves."

Win told *Billboard*: "It gave us such a control over our own future that we are very fortunate to have. I don't judge anyone for wanting to take the money to be able to make the records you want to make. We had a very unusual situation."

Arcade Fire performing during the first night of their residency at St John's Church in Westminster, on January 29, 2007 in London. JIM DYSON/GETTY IMAGES

Richard Parry performs on stage at Mt Smart Stadium on January 18, 2008 in Auckland, New Zealand. HANNAH JOHNSTON/GETTY IM

On stage at the Big Day Out at Sydney Olympic Park on January 25, 2008 in Australia. HEADPRESS/RETNA PICTURES

Brothers in arms: Win and William Butler at a Barack Obama rally at Beachland Ballroom on March 3, 2008 in Cleveland, Ohio.
KEVIN MAZUR/WIREIMAGE

Sarah Neufeld at Lollapalooza 2010 at Grant Park in Chicago. MICHAEL TRAVIS/CORBIS

Win Butler at Madison Square Garden in New York City on August 4, 2010. JOE KOHEN/WIREIMAGE FOR NEW YORK POST

Regine at The O2 Arena, London, Britain, December 1 2010. BRIAN RASIC/REX FEATURES

Onstage at the Philipshalle on November 29, 2010 in Duesseldorf, Germany. PETER WAFZIG/GETTY IMAGES

Cyndi Lauper (centre) joins Arcade Fire during the 2011 New Orleans Jazz & Heritage Festival Day 5 at The Fair Grounds Race Course in New Orleans on May 6, 2011. RICK DIAMOND/GETTY IMAGES

Win Butler at the Austin City Limits Music Festival Day Three at Zilker Park in Austin, Texas on September 18, 2011.
TIM MOSENFELDER/GETTY IMAGES

Win Butler (L) performs with Mavis Staples (R) at the Lands End Stage during the 2011 Outside Lands Music And Arts Festival at Golden Gate Park in San Francisco, California on August 14, 2011. JEFF KRAVITZ/GETTY IMAGES

'Helpless' Tim Kingsbury, Neil Young, and Win Butler perform as part of the 25th Annual Bridge School Benefit at Shoreline Amphitheatre in Mountain View, California on October 22, 2011. TIM MOSENFELDER/GETTY IMAGES

Controversial winners! Arcade Fire accept Album of the Year award for *The Suburbs* onstage during The 53rd Annual Grammy Awards held at Staples Center on February 13, 2011 in Los Angeles, California. KEVIN WINTER/GETTY IMAGES

Arcade Fire winner international group and album award. The Brit Awards, Press Room, O2 Arena, London, Britain on February 15, 2011. DAVID FISHER/REX FEATURES

Will Butler on their Tour For The Suburbs, St. Louis, America, April 2, 2011. STARTRAKS PHOTO/REX FEATURES

Chapter 13

Arcade Fire And Haiti

It seems rather obvious to point out that the link between Arcade Fire and Haiti began with Régine Chassagne. The traumas suffered by her family, their friends and compatriots during the Duvalier period have shaped her world-view and fired her with a passion to help her true native land. How could it have affected her otherwise? The dark shadow of Duvalier lay heavily over her childhood days and, naturally, the depth and fire of this passion would affect not just Win Butler but the other members of Arcade Fire. The connection seeped deeply into the band's psyche in so many ways. One may naturally take the song 'Haiti' as the starting point, and so it was. But the song was more than a mere sad reflection on a nation's troubled history, it served as a declaration of intent, not just for Chassagne, but for the entire band. Arcade Fire has always been aware of the pitfalls of being seen as yet another rock band earning kudos and credibility by performing high-level benefit gigs.

Win Butler has spoken about the issue in *Trouser Press* magazine: "It has been difficult for us to convey the depth of emotion that we, collectively, have for the Haitian people. I am not saying that giant events like Live Aid were a bad thing... in fact I don't know but I am sure they achieved much. But with us and in this instance, we are not merely performing on some benefit day. Haiti tends to affect everything we do. It's there all the time and it is not something that will ever go away."

One can read this many ways but there is no doubt that Haiti is deeply ingrained with the music – given Régine's continuing Haitian music explorations – and within Win Butler's lyricism, that can often be linked, if in metaphorical sense, with the stricken country. This link was firmly structured within the basic ethos of Arcade Fire even before the devastating earthquake struck in 2010. Naturally, in the wake of that disaster and, frankly, the often bewildering politics that have surrounded aid and rebuilding programmes, the band's desire to offer positive, tangible and practical help has intensified considerably.

The show at Hyde Park offered practical proof of this with one dollar or euro from every ticket sold going directly to a number of aid organisations at work in Haiti. However, one organisation in particular, Partners In Health, has benefited from close links with the band. During the course of 2011, Arcade Fire ticket buyers donated more than $300,000 to the organisation with £60,000 coming from the Hyde Park show alone.

Speaking to *Mother Jones* magazine, Régine reflected on the source of her links with Haiti: "Before I met Win, I was a university student working two or three jobs, so I didn't have the time or money to do anything about Haiti. In the beginning of the band, all my efforts were in trying to make music. After completing our first record, I started realising that this adventure was going to bring in a decent income, so instantly I started to think about sharing this success with Haiti. In 2004, we played two hometown shows and gave all the profits to Albert Schweitzer's hospital in Haiti. A couple of months later, I read the book *Mountains Beyond Mountains* by Tracy Kidder and discovered the work of an incredible organization called Partners In Health, founded by Dr. Paul Farmer. Since then, we've been working together in many different ways."

Win Butler: "Once I got to know what's been happening historically, it's pretty impossible to un-know it. Like right now, there's the outbreak of cholera in Haiti, and people see that as a news headline, but I know there's half a billion dollars of aid that one senator is putting a hold on, that the Red Cross has raised half a billion dollars but has only spent $200 million. If I was a cabinetmaker or a commercial fisherman, it would be the same question – how to connect to my world. The job we do affords us the opportunity to have people listen to what we say. But a lot of people have a similar situation: they're trying to find a way to do some good."

Speaking to *The Observer,* Win said: "One point of our trip to Haiti was to see how this money is being used. Partners In Health works all over the world. In Haiti, PIH and its sister organisation Zanmi Lasante [Partners In Health in Creole] employs more than 5,000 Haitians. There are some non-Haitian employees and foreign volunteers – visiting orthopedic surgeons, engineers – but the vast majority of the doctors and nurses are Haitian, as are the construction workers, janitors, community health workers, secretaries and so on.

"One thing I learned was that PIH employs lots of construction workers. They are building a large teaching hospital in the town of Mirebalais [the biggest construction project begun in Haiti since the earthquake]. The main result will be access to high-level medical care for the 140,000 people living in the region, but employment is an intended side effect. Haitians do the construction as far as possible. Where locals are unskilled – in plumbing, electrical wiring, welding – foreign volunteers are brought in to work and help train. John Chew, the project co-ordinator, was excited about how his bricklayers could now read blueprints – a good, marketable skill. When people have jobs, other people can sell them cell phones or, hey, bootlegged DVDs. The economy slowly grows. This is happening not just in Mirebalais but also with smaller clinics and schools PIH is building throughout rural Haiti.

"Health, as you might assume, is the main concern of PIH. They are known and celebrated for their successful treatment of Aids and TB patients in extremely poor regions. But they take a broad view of health. One employee talked about digitising medical records and seeing several prescriptions for 'needs new roof'. And these prescriptions had been filled. We met Genevieve Joubert, a nurse who lives and works in the tent camp of Dadadou in Port-au-Prince. She has helped deliver more than 150 babies since the earthquake. But she also focuses on latrines – on the struggle to find someone to build more. And on the more infuriating struggle to get someone to regularly empty them. The people who work for Partners In Health work there for the same reason any of us would. Some work just because they need a job. Most seem to strongly believe in PIH's vision. The doctors and nurses could get higher pay working for other foreign organisations, or the UN. Many, with foreign graduate degrees, could get jobs anywhere in the world. Dr Patrick Almazor is from Port-au-Prince and a former Fulbright scholar with a master's degree in public health. He runs the hospital in St Marc, a coastal town where cholera hit particularly hard last year. He'd started with PIH because of a mandatory year of service post-medical school. He'd stayed because he realised he wanted to serve the poor, and he found working with PIH was the best way to do that.

"PIH are breathtakingly competent," Win added. "I would describe them as efficient, but that might imply a focus on cost-effectiveness and the system, instead of on the patient. I'd rather say that PIH are thorough in all aspects of operation and wise in their use of money and supplies. They are part of a strong, organic movement towards a functioning society in Haiti".

As if Haiti hadn't been through enough, disaster struck on Tuesday, January 12, 2010 at seven minutes to ten in the evening. At this precise moment a powerful earthquake of 7.0 magnitude struck Haiti at a depth of 8.1 miles. It was the most powerful earthquake to hit the area since 1770. The epicentre was located 15 miles west south west of Port-au-Prince. It is difficult to imagine a more devastatingly placed quake though the fear of such an event is something that Haitians have lived with for many years. However, the desperate political situations and the sheer struggle to exist ensured that the possibility of a quake of such magnitude and its aftermath remained in the background.

And that wasn't all. Following the initial quake came 59 aftershocks, some of which ranged between 4.2 to 5.9 magnitude in strength. Had they occurred singularly, they would have been immensely serious shocks in their own right. The Haitian Government estimates that over 200,000 people died as a result of the quake and subsequent aftershocks.

In addition, at least a further 2,000,000 were left homeless and over 3,000,000 were in need of emergency aid and, while an estimated $575 million was collected via agencies such as the World Food Programme and UNICEF – with over 3,000,000 meals delivered to 200,000 people – the figure fell far short of a relief effort that could be considered successful.

While tons of aid have been delivered to Haiti so far, it isn't nearly enough considering that three million people there need food and water. Despite a complex array of donations from countries and individual companies from around the globe, conspiracy theories abound in the wake of a global effort that doesn't stretch far enough.

But whatever the political facts, one truth remained. The situation was desperate and Arcade Fire's links with Haiti had now taken on much higher emotive proportions. Benefit concerts, however big, would no longer be enough. The band had to become involved with the people of the country in long-lasting and continually effective ways.

Although Arcade Fire remain prolific bloggers – see arcadefire.com for regular updates – in regard to Haitian trips, endeavours and aid links, arguably the most poignant example came from the diaryesque jottings of Régine Chassagne, writing about the band's trip to the country in the summer of 2011, which were published in *The Observer*, and parts of which are represented below. They stem from the band's decision to perform at the remote mountain town of Cange.

Régine and the band were welcomed into the late afternoon sun by a perfectly calligraphed banner that proclaimed: "Bienvenue a Cange, Régine et Win, Arcade Fire". The village had a medieval feel, as if carved out of the mountains, lush and full of trees, as Régine explained: "The trees that were planted 25 years ago when the NGO we work with, Partners In Health (PIH), began work here have now grown into a landscape hinting at Haiti's luxurious forests of the past. But Cange – PIH's headquarters in Haiti – is definitely one step into the future as it springs out of dry mountains, organised, filled with Haitian nurses and doctors, electricity and paved roads. You can see that the town has been built in phases over the years, up and down the hill, in and around large medieval-looking metal gates. This makes Cange's unusual charm."

The trip, in 2011, was the third time Régine had visited the town. However, although she had previously met the folks while accompanied by Win, this would mark the band's first full-scale appearance in the country. It was a truly warming – literally, as temperatures soared – experience for the band. As if in a sobering flashback to the days before success softened the rigours of performing life, in Haiti, the band started to unload the equipment themselves.

The small town had certainly pulled out all the stops by assembling a wooden stage on a dusty, sun-scorched football field close to the town centre sporting a second welcoming banner. The gig was genuinely pushing at the boundaries of live rock music. Indeed, with resources at the Central Plateau at an all-time low, the prospect of a live music evening was undoubtedly the largest event ever held in the region and anticipation ran high.

Roy Harper, the legendary Irish-based Mancunian folk singer, once noted how easy it was to tell when you are in a poor country. In a poor country, on a hot sunny day, the entire town would congregate in some central area, be it a town square or park. Music and dancing would strike up and everyone – parents, children, drunks and even the dogs – would get off on the vibe that it was absolutely free. In a rich country this only happens after tickets have been purchased and consumerism taps into a vibe that should, by rights, be free for everyone. In this instance, Arcade Fire, a band from the rich west, would be taking their version of western consumer music and turning it on its head for the benefit of the people.

One curious incident occurred when Win Butler, perhaps high on the village ramshackle DIY vibe, attempted to make a makeshift drum for the performance out of two red plastic wastebaskets he found near the gates of a clinic. They had an abandoned look about them and Win dumped one inside the other and started thumping it experimentally. Pleased with his handiwork, he handed it to Jeremy Gara, a more experienced percussionist who, after vigorously thumping it, also agreed about its percussive qualities. The idea would be to use the drum for a rendition of 'Windowsill' during the gig. It was only when they moved it to the stage site with the other equipment that someone noticed the warning label on the side of the drum. "Biohazard Medical Waste" it rather threateningly proclaimed. The baskets were duly returned to their rightful place and ideas of experimental percussion were abandoned, for this gig at least.

But there is no doubt that, for the band, the gig proved a chastening experience. Plugging their instruments in for the somewhat ramshackle soundcheck was certainly a deflating experience as no electricity arrived to power any of their amps. The Haitian soundman, unflummoxed and unhurried, wandered over to the gas-powered generator, literally kicking it into action. Régine noted that the sound, when it actually arrived, was "… actually better than the sound we had on the *Funeral* tour". Big tarpaulins were used to cover the equipment as dark storm clouds wavered.

Régine Chassagne's blog noted: "In the meantime, a small bus enters through the Cange gates. RAM is here. We have played with this Haitian band a few times now and we are happy to see that they, too, made it safely on time. They opened for us once in Quebec City, but here in Haiti we are definitely the support band. Caribbean showers rarely last for long. So we decide to take the opportunity to all go for dinner. We walk down the hill to the small community centre that is the one room large enough to accommodate us all. I can tell that the cooking staff have been working all day, if not all week, in preparation. The table is set for a banquet. Goat and chicken, plantain, two kinds of rice, salad, rum cake… Last time we were here, it was rice and beans for lunch and peanut-butter sandwiches for dinner. One of the staff tells us a story about a funeral for a young man that had taken place a few days earlier. During some recent funerals people had become so riled in their grief they'd broken several metal folding chairs (at around 500 Haitian gourdes or £7.60 each). The priest, Father Lafontant told everyone during the last eulogy that anyone breaking a chair during the service would have to pay for it, and sure enough he had to point to two people during the service and yell out: 'Cinq-cent gourdes!'"

The link between Arcade Fire and RAM was forged on the previous summer when RAM had been invited to Quebec City to perform on the same bill. During the course of that weekend, many friendships were made. It was somewhat imbalanced, however, as the RAM musicians looked at the Quebec Festival VIP catering tent in a state of awe. Cleary they had never seen such lavish displays of food before. Arcade Fire duly noted that the Haitian musicians were, themselves, still living in dilapidated tents that had been erected in Port-au-Prince in the wake of the previous year's earthquake. Feeling humbled at the comparison, Arcade Fire instantly resolved to work harder, to do more to make a genuine and tangible difference.

Régine continued: "I am grateful that they are with us tonight. As part of the evening program we also invited a man called Ti Zwazo (Little Bird) to come and sing for the crowd. He is a part of Zanmi Agrikol, PIH's agricultural project. Back in 2008, as we were visiting his sapling farm, he sang two of the most beautiful songs I'd ever heard. Joan, a PIH staffer called him the day before and left a message on his mobile. (Everybody has a phone in Haiti. They might not have a house or enough to eat, but somehow phones spring up everywhere.) Little Bird called back leaving a most solemn message: 'Hello. This is Ti Zwazo. I understand you need my services to sing at a concert tomorrow night. Thank you for thinking of me. I would like to notify you that it will be my pleasure to perform at your concert. Merci et au revoir.' The fancy French expressions I hear around Cange amaze me. Brought into a 2011 context, they turn any mundane conversation into sophisticated 18th-century court talk. It blows my mind to hear a 13-year-old ask me about the simplest thing using language that probably would have appeared normal to Shakespeare. It is surreal. I love it. Ti Zwazo arrives, all shaven, in a pressed shirt and tie – quite a change from the second-hand T-shirt and straw hat he was wearing when we met him three years ago. Has it been three years? He stands in a corner, all shy. I get off my seat and insist he comes to sit and eat with us. Ti Zwazo's face is the one of a rugged middle-aged farmer, his eyes are sharp with wisdom, but in this unfamiliar context he sits down and eats silently like a timid schoolboy."

Before the gig, the band had to walk up a shady hill to the gig arena. A crowd had started to form, literally drifting down from the hills. People on foot, people in cars, pouring into the town. People started to congregate, sitting on walls, hanging around, enjoying the vibe, in precisely the manner described by Roy Harper. The band still had to soundcheck and, not wishing to destroy the mystique, they kept it short, just concentrating on one song. They were pretty confident as the soundman from the Port–au–Prince gig, two days earlier, had travelled along to oversee the gig. Nevertheless, it must have seemed a strange scenario for a band that had been performing in some of the largest arenas on the world circuit. But here, in Haiti, they appeared to be – literally – walking into the heart of their spiritual home.

The build-up to the gig is beautifully outlined here, by Régine: "The sun has finally set. John, one of PIH's few non-Haitian staff arrives with yellow construction lamps as makeshift stage lighting. The evening is about to start. Down comes the night's busy bee, cheery and driven Marie-Flore, the daughter of Father Lafontant. She's the one behind all this welcoming protocol: 'We need you to go on stage and stand in line please. Somebody is going to introduce you.' So we do as we're told. The next minutes look like a surreal inauguration. The youth of Cange has formed a marching band and is walking towards us. 'Ladies and gentlemen, please welcome from Canada, Arcade and Fire. Please, clap for Régine, please clap for her husband Win, clap for Tim, clap for Jeremy, clap for Richard, clap for Sarah, clap for Marika, clap for manager Scott! And now allow us to play for you the Canadian national anthem!' You'd have to have a heart of stone to remain unmoved by the gigantic effort this community had put forward. I notice that the students are playing the very instruments Win and I brought them last August. 'They've gotten so good!' I whisper to Win. I can't believe how much they've improved! They must have been practising a ton!

"And now, please oblige us as we play our own anthem, *La Dessalinienne!*"

Following this introduction, Régine and the band stepped down from the stage to allow the local solo artist, Ti Zwazo, to take the stage. He was the kind of musician who could easily have assembled a band and allowed himself to sit back a little, but that wouldn't have been his style. Gifted with a voice that Régine described as 'pure gold', he played a ferocious set with a sound that reverberated fuzzily off the stone walls across the soccer field. A warning, perhaps, for Arcade Fire, whose giant sound could easily be lost in such circumstances. However, other than covering all the walls with rugs, there didn't seem to be anything they could physically do. No such trouble for Ti Zwazo, who sings hastily scribbled songs about Arcade Fire's arrival in Cange and the need for the country to "come together", with Haitians and non-Haitians pitching in to help with the rebuilding. It was a rallying call and the perfect example of the sheer power of music. Free music.

"For all farmers here tonight! You here?" he asked.

The farmers cheered approvingly, collectively accepting the limelight.

"For all the mechanics here tonight!" Mechanics cheered.

"We've got to put our heads together, for a better Haiti…"

His powerful song came to a finale with his last soaring note drowned by thunderous cheers.

Régine wondered how many other Ti Zwazos the country might hold, singing alone in the night when the lights are out. It is the fear of many successful musicians who have emulated rather than imitated music forms from humble origins. Indeed, the title of 1998 Jimmy Page and Robert Plant album, *Walking Into Clarksdale*, adheres to that very feeling, how humbling it is when a multi-millionaire rock superstar is confronted by equal if not greater talents performing on street corners. Led Zeppelin's 'Clarksdale And Deep South' is Arcade Fire's 'Haiti'. However talented the individual performers within Arcade Fire might be, when confronted by music in such a way, they are forced to secretly admit that luck and placement in the scheme of things have played such a huge part in their success. It is certainly a healthy way of arresting the rampant ego. All rock stars, perhaps, should be forced to recognise this.

Eventually it was time for Arcade Fire to take the stage and they duly launched into a joyous rendition of 'Keep The Car Running'. The scene before them unfolded politely, rather than exploding in western mosh-pit style. Some of those who had been sitting on the rear stone wall immediately hopped off and sidled down to the front. The first song sealed the success of the gig, any tension neatly draining away. Not a bad achievement considering the town has never hosted a concert of this kind before not had any exposure whatsoever to the dynamics of a modern-day rock concert.

Régine continued: "We're happy to see people appear genuinely happy about the music. So we play our hearts out. No super fans, no journalists. Just us, the townspeople, Ti Zwazo and RAM. As we play the song 'Haiti', I invite Philemond, one of the older youths of Cange, to come on stage. In 2008 he sang the song with Win and me, and has learned it on the guitar since. We're out of guitars, but it doesn't matter. He starts to sing front and centre and leads the singing crowd. The sun has finally set. John, one of PIH's few non-Haitian staff arrives with yellow construction lamps as makeshift stage lighting. The evening is about to start. Surprisingly, everything sounds good on stage. No feedbacks, everything is clear. We definitely have had worse sound in fancier places. By the end of the show a good number of people are jumping, hands in the air, all smiles. I think we've made new friends."

The set was more than a triumph, more than a rock show, more than an across the seas connection, even. After playing two sets, the band was encircled by grateful youngsters, close to tears, telling the band they "had never seen anything like it before".

If anything, the Port-au-Prince show (on March 29), was more interesting, if not in terms of venue then certainly in regard to the number of unlikely cover versions that sparkled from their one-off set. In direct contrast to the outdoor event, the Port-au-Prince show was secretive, impromptu and as intimate as any of their shows since the days of the Montreal house parties.

The gig took place within the complex of the capital's Hotel Oloffson, in a comparatively tiny room lined with a bar and, apparently, a row of stools on which sat wholly bemused drinkers who, no doubt, had made it down to the bar intent on catching some well-deserved relaxation after a day of relief work.

The band's choice of cover versions for this night would have made sure that any bootleg recording would have attained legendary status. A stomping, rather weirdly celebratory 'Girls Just Wanna Have Fun' saw them taking on the visual attack of The Scissor Sisters – seven musicians lost in an orgy of arm waving, spinning and mock-disco dancing. It did seem an odd choice and, indeed, no Haitian link can be traced but, perhaps, if any city in the world deserved a few minutes of sheer mindless fun, it would be Port-au-Prince.

Next came a song that was closely associated with the spirit of a nation that had suffered so much over the years: John Fogerty's Creedence Clearwater Revival classic 'Who'll Stop The Rain?' It was a song that Win Butler had played many times in pre-Arcade Fire rehearsals, basically as a way of finding his way around a classic rock number. Will Butler then took the lead vocals spot for a rousing run-through of The Rolling Stones' 'The Last Time', another song that might be said to capture the spirit of the said nation.

The significance of the hotel is also worth a mention. It is owned by Richard Morse, leader of the band RAM. Win Butler, in particular, had expressed a desire to help to produce a video for RAM, in order to help them achieve wider recognition, one more string of the myriad links between the band and the country.

Basking in the wake of such a successful night led the band to something of an anti-climax on the following day. Cange had returned to some kind of dreamy normality, the stage was being carefully dismantled and an air of pragmatism had settled on the town. It was strangely sad, with the band falling back into the tedium of being a touring band. They took a fairly uneventful trip back into Port-au-Prince and then onto the airport where they faced an eight-hour wait. Just one of the regular stretches of tedium that is synonymous with touring. Half of the band flew directly into JFK in order to be present at the final LCD Soundsystem show at Madison Square Garden. The danger in this, despite the friendship with LCD, was that it could have seemed like such an enormous culture shock. From playing with and seeing RAM perform in the dust, to all the razzle-dazzle of a big-time rock concert. But, as Will Butler noted in his online blog: "It actually felt related to see LCD play and watch New York go crazy. It was refreshing to see music not just be entertainment, but be actually meaningful to these wildly different communities. And there was decent dancing at both events."

Chapter 14

The Crowds That Gather

Hyde Park, June 30, 2011

There was a rumble in my phone on the previous day. A slight childish thrill hit me as I noticed the name Dounia Mikou – from the Arcade Fire management office – on the tag. But the message, though welcoming, curiously upbeat even, explained the frenetic nature of the current tour and no Hyde Park meeting would be possible. It wasn't too crushing a disappointment, for the next sentence suggested a meeting in Manchester, perhaps the aesthetic heart of this band and the perfect venue, come late August, where I envisaged guiding them around the music ghosts of the city, the now bland yet pristine bunches of stylish flats, where grubby venues used to sit and hold the local music so darkly, so effectively. As Arcade Fire would be performing at the soulless concrete shell of the MEN Arena – a deadening basketball arena, ugly and horribly wedged next to the still evocative Victoria railway station – I longed to take them out of that unholy shell, and let them drift through the old city, the pubs and streets of inspiring industrial character.

So, Manchester it would be, hopefully, and, happy with this possibility, I allowed myself to sink back into the role of fan, content to drift into a steamy London day, looking forward to the 'gig'.

Hyde Park in the late afternoon was populated by garishly clad joggers, amblers and, sitting on benches by the Serpentine like ageing characters from John Le Carré, besuited men crumpling through *The Daily Telegraph*.

Somewhat oddly, there appeared to be no sign of a gig... of 60,000 people gathered for the strains of New York's gypsy funksters Beirut, of posh boy pop punksters The Vaccines, arguably the year's biggest British breakthrough, and their close friends, Mumford and Sons, whose twee folk pop and Victorian apparel had rather passed me by.

In truth, myself and partner, Vicky, were only there for one reason... one band and, most importantly, a band launching into the biggest and most significant non-festival appearance of their career.

The absurdity of their previous collective persona – 'a band with no hits' – already rendered obsolete by the stock of instantly accessible songs at their disposal and, in purely practical terms, by the post-*Suburbs* genuine hit, 'Speaking In Tongues', which, by now, had lodged on every mainstream radio show in Britain, even to the dubious point of becoming omnipresent on Radio Two. Would the band be forced to shed their artistic integrity beyond this point as so many had before? Probably not, but the savage tug of the mainstream was starting to cause major problems.

But not at Hyde Park, and a classic little corner of Hyde Park, squarely ticked near Bayswater Road (we found it, in the end, by following the drifting throng of excitable Mumford and Sons fans over the Serpentine), and a perfectly encapsulated mini-festival in the shadow of the previous week's Glastonbury. Square perimeter, polite, guiding security and, as expected, ever-so-trendified middle-class audience politely soaking up the vibe. Relieved, too, that the sombre threat of the afternoon's storm clouds had receded and, in glorious contrast to the well-documented Glastonbury deluge, a beautiful evening dawned.

It would be difficult to think of a less stressful occasion. Thankfully, the relaxed vibe which seemed to positively affect every one of the 50,000 attendees, didn't seem to add the kind of family-soaked blandness that – in truth – had started to polish away the essential edge of many British festivals, including and especially Latitude. While one would be hard-pressed to find an edge, there was an excitability that seemed almost childlike, especially as anticipation levels rose to greet the opening mock-cinematic scenes, pulled from the Spike Jonze extended film, *Scenes From The Suburbs*, based on the feel and atmosphere of the album. The childlike excitability certainly affected the mood of the band, who fell on the stage with tumble-clown glee; beaming smiles and thankful waves.

"We are just pleased it is such a beautiful evening," said Win. "We saw those storm clouds rolling in this afternoon and feared the worst."

By the second song, the glorious, rousing 'Wake Up', the audience was lifted to joyous, arm flailing, singing, screaming celebration that saw knots of appalling dad-dancing breaking out across the arena. This seemed like an effortless homecoming for the band to their – musically speaking – adopted isle. Even that ultra-infectious hit single, 'Speaking In Tongues', with its charming laid-back simplicity, failed to soften this unlikely exuberance and one felt, at all times, that the gig carried with it a certain historical kudos. Never mind the fact that, the previous week, the same venue had hosted The Killers (often linked with Arcade Fire, if only for semi-religious reasons) and, three days later, the triumphant return of the universally beloved Pulp. And many bands in recent years – The Foo Fighters – had achieved similar excitable results in the same venue. Despite all this, one couldn't help but allow the mind to wander back to Tony Palmer's iconic *Stones In The Park* film, which saw Mick Jagger release a flock of butterflies in tribute to Brian Jones. Or, for that matter, the brief mating of the extraordinary talents of Eric Clapton and Stevie Winwood in the ill-fated supergroup Blind Faith.

Arcade Fire's 90 minutes zipped by in a flash, and seemed testament to a repertoire that is now three albums deep and large enough to fill such a space without repetition. But everything you wished for was stacked into the set: 'No Cars Go', 'Rebellion (Lies)', 'Rococo', 'The Suburbs', all hummable, swaying rhythms that would still be swilling around the heads of the crowd as they tucked into their breakfasts the following morning.

The stage, minuscule from any attainable viewpoint, we found, was enhanced by giant screens of portrait and landscape nature and, most important of all, a beautifully lit set that even softened neatly in tandem with the darkening evening. Diehard festival-goers will all have seen how frustrating this can be when the simple logistics of creating intimacy via big screen fail to add to the evocative nature of the event, as is mostly the case. Here, the effect was to drive an intimacy into the occasion; even if the sight of giant Canadians could be faintly intimidating, it carried the onstage vitality to the rear of the arena, to the point of capturing onstage looks of delight and, occasionally, a touch of nervousness – Sarah Neufeld fumbling for the violin, Will forgetting the words and Régine flashing red knickers, big and bold, before 50,000 pairs of eyes.

If there was a trace – and just a trace – of eventual disappointment, it might have been the non appearance of a 'special guest'; a Bowie or Byrne would have been a cherry for the occasion, but it mattered not, with the crowd effortlessly dispersing down the Bayswater and Edgware Roads, snaking back to hotels and Underground, the sound of Win Butler screaming "We will see you in two years," still ringing in their ears.

Four days after the Hyde Park appearance came the emergence of the Spike Jonze-directed *Scenes From The Suburbs*, a half-hour visualisation of – presumably – his personal take on the Grammy-winning album or, at least, the feelings that bounce around his head while allowing the textures to seep fully in. Consider a typical American suburban estate – in this case Austin, Texas – full of cycling, snogging, chortling, swearing fop-kids, swelled by parental money, edged by similar expectation and allowed to dream hard dreams in a soft environment. Jonze grabbed 'real' kids for the film, snatching them from the local high school and hurtling them into the fray of filmmaking. This ruse worked, allowing a natural exuberance to flavour a film that, on one level, is about the traditional teenage emotional surges, sexual awakening, jealousy, the flood of love and desire, the terror of growing into a world. Nothing, really, that you wouldn't find in *American Graffiti* – and how odd to see the American suburbs still retaining that fifties sheen, despite the upgrade in both housing and automobiles, still that wave of pastel-coloured silence remains in silent streets housing so many emotive secrets, with interlocking lives, loves, hates, secret liaisons and casual feuding. How teenage experience always tapped into the suppressed emotion of their safe, aloof if unsophisticated parents; the lie of the everyday idyll, the suppressive pretence of normality, the Stepford smiles, the creep of evil that forms behind blandness. The artless existence of car-washing, fridge buying, weekending norm, father beer drinking to the football, mother hitting the sherry circuits and confused offspring affecting niceness while running wild within their inner circle of cider parties and reckless fucking. The conservative escapes of drink and prescription drugs, burgers, metal and hip-hop. Gawky lads lost in juvenile daftness, pretty girls surprised to be empowered by sexuality and advanced intelligence, unskilfully causing chaos in their wake, hurtling here, there and everywhere.

Expand this vision, as Jonze does, and you may find warring suburban tribes. Expand further and border fences are erected and patrolled, Governmental control wades in, blackly clad and battering with indiscriminate hate. The full force of official violence is unleashed in the film, rather than hidden (as in the real world). All Jonze is doing is releasing the true emotions that flood the suburbs. That, perhaps, is the perfect expression of the album. No surprise then to find that the Butler brothers enjoy co-writing credits – with Win affecting the narration – and allowing this film to exist as a genuine and illuminating extension of the album itself. No demystification involved, indeed, one run-through of the film sends the viewer spinning back to the album, to uncover emotions previously unleashed. To enjoy a greater understanding of the songwriting and its 'feel'.

The film was released on DVD as an attachment to an upgraded release of *The Suburbs* album. This might have annoyed completists locked into the need to own everything, although the low price (£9.99 in HMV) bizarrely set this two-disc affair below the official single album, at least in some retail outlets. There was more, too. In a second attached film, *The Making Of The Suburbs*, the teen actors are unleashed in all their nascent glory, spilling the often rather crass daftness of studenthood here and there, literally before the apparently accepting eyes of Arcade Fire. Picture a scene where one student is telling a gory tale of excessive consumption – like any student night on any campus in the world – and Will and Régine creasing in a laughter which I sense to be genuine. It is a brave glimpse beyond any aura of cool that might have been constructed and how nice to see it there.

Best of all is the battle between wonderment and boredom that often flashes across the faces of the teenage actors, whether on set and under pressure or flicking through scripts, lost in the realisation that such an honour will also require a considerable amount of concentration and hard work. It works best not merely as a companion piece to the film, but as a brief glimpse into the hard-working heart of the band and their determination to see a project through to completion.

Scenes From The Suburbs also reflects the fading eighties phenomenon of expanding a song, a single, into an elastic 12-inch version, allowing the producer, rather than the band in most cases, to stretch a track beyond its natural limits and into – more often than not – a wholly danceable and unrelated 'part two'. The Thompson Twins parallel might be furthered here, as Jonze teases *The Suburbs* to a new cinematic level.

The *Scenes From The Suburbs* DVD arrived in the music shops in the form of a deluxe version of *The Suburbs*, complete with booklet, the album and two extra songs. Just enough, given the low pricing, to make it a worthwhile purchase even if the album was already in your collection or, indeed, as an MP3. The two extra songs, 'Culture War' and the already hugely familiar 'Speaking In Tongues' don't necessarily exist as seamless additions to *The Suburbs* and are best treated as the lonely 'add ons' they effectively are.

'Culture War' is a brash song of changing times. Win Butler reaches back to his Bible-reading days, hoping for some ancient wisdom to nullify the heady rush into digital technology that has completely traumatised the record industry. Taking on the role of "soldiers in a culture war" might sound slightly pretentious, but it is a good take on the ethos of Arcade Fire, given their multi-instrumental takes on just about everything that brings history – literally – screaming into the present. In this respect Arcade Fire is a blast from the past yet wholly contemporary. There is a danger, of course, that artists can become lost in the rush of technology and feed the machine instead of trusting their own intuition. That is the gauntlet thrown down and, as noble as it might seem, Arcade Fire – among others, of course – are leading the fight to cling to an ancient and organic artistic wisdom. Films are all but gone, lost to special effects and the exodus from cinemas into home entertainment centres, if not mobile phones. The concept of the album seemingly shattered into modern-day cherry-picking which sees songs arrive with absolutely no sense of context at all. All may be lost in this dizzying rush.

"You want it, you got it, here's your culture war... tell us what it is for."

Good question. At the very heart of technology lies nothing. And, if nothing else, Arcade Fire exist to punch aesthetic realism into that vacuous space, into the very heart of technology. If that is arrogance, I will take it over Katy Perry and Lady Gaga, any day.

'Speaking In Tongues', the song that finally broke Arcade Fire's ill-fitting 'band without a hit' status, became one of the key soundtrack recordings of 2011. Indeed, its effortless driving quality is sufficient for it to entice the mind for months on end and, as mentioned, soft and pliable enough to climb gently onto mainstream radio. One will forever expect it to conclude with Ken Bruce 'back announcing' his link into the 11 o'clock news.

Taking its title from the 1983 Talking Heads album (which included 'Burning Down The House', 'Making Flippy Floppy' and 'Slippery People') and featuring David Byrne on backing vocals, it is a sideways tribute to one of Win Butler's acknowledged key influences. Not that you would know this from the song itself or, indeed, it's slight lyrical wordplay.

"Come out of your head and into the world now," pleads Butler as the song slides to its lovely conclusion. Indeed, only the harsh opening line "Hypocrite reader" seems to contain any trace of Butler's trademark measured angst. Nevertheless, it's a beautiful song capable of changing the atmosphere in an instant.

Late summer, 2011, saw Arcade Fire finally winding down to the close of the extensive *Suburbs* tour. While many, in England at least, regarded the Hyde Park gig as their ultimate live achievement, one festival appearance across the English Channel seemed to upstage even that. Unlike at Hyde Park, Arcade Fire were in this instance forced to work an initially unresponsive crowd assembled not just to see them but for many acts.

The gig in question was The Main Square Festival in the Citadel in the north French town of Arras, a European crossroads equidistant between Brussels, Paris and London where many communication roads meet. Built between 1667 and 1672 after Vauban's plans, the Citadel is listed among the UNESCO world heritage sites. In 2010, the Main Square Festival was established in the heart of a 40-hectare park located very near the town centre. Thanks to the 10-hectare area of the Citadel, this vast place offers the artists and the public exceptional conditions for enjoying great shows in a magnificent setting.

Arcade Fire's Arras performance has been regarded by many as one of the key moments of their career insofar as they took the festival by the scruff of the neck and made it their own. Notwithstanding the efforts of no lesser rock names than Coldplay, Moby, Linkin Park, Kasabian and Liam Gallagher's new band, Beady Eye, it was Arcade Fire who stole the show despite an initially unresponsive crowd, which inspired Win Butler to launch into a stream of crowd-baiting rhetoric. It certainly seemed to do the trick as anthem followed anthem in the Arcade Fire tradition. The set – 'Ready To Start', 'Keep The Car Running'. 'No Cars Go', 'Haiti', 'Intervention', 'Suburban War', 'Rococo', 'Speaking In Tongues', 'The Suburbs', 'The Suburbs Continued', 'Month Of May', 'Neighborhood II (Laika)', 'Neighborhood I (Tunnels)', 'Rebellion (Lies)' and encores of 'Wake Up' and 'Sprawl II (Mountains Beyond Mountains')' – seems impregnable in terms of sheer aural bombardment. For the moment, the Arcade Fire live experience retains a sense of relentlessness that bludgeons any apathetic crowd into submission.

On September 22, 2011, the band proudly returned to play what was billed as 'a very big show' to mark the 10th anniversary of the Pop Montreal Festival. Television company SiriusXM Canada presented and broadcasted the free outdoor show by Arcade Fire at the Place des Festivals of Quartier des Spectacles in downtown Montreal.

The show was regarded as a 'grand thank you' by Arcade Fire to Montreal, Quebec and Canada and before a huge body of fans in their homeland they duly celebrated an unprecedented year of success, touring the world in support of *The Suburbs* and collecting awards at the Junos, the Brits and the Grammys.

Commenting in the run-up to the gig, Régine stated: "Our band couldn't exist without Montreal. After having had the chance to tour extensively around the world, we're very excited to finally come home. And to do so the Montreal way, we hoped to play a free outside show, on the very last day of summer as a big 'thank you' to the beautiful city we love so much.

"We're happy to be a part of the 10th anniversary of Pop Montreal. And we're proud to play a role in the French release of Tracy Kidder's *Mountains Beyond Mountains (Soulever Les Montagnes)* – a book that has influenced our lives and our careers. Hoping to see you at the show... we're crossing our fingers for great weather."

Montreal outfit Karkwa, the 2010 Polaris Prize winners, opened an event that seemed unique in that it saw the collective media and government powers of the city pulling together in a spirit of celebration. It is difficult to imagine a parallel situation anywhere in Europe as the funders, partners and sponsors included SiriusXM Canada, Quartier des Spectacles Partnership, Agence Métropolitaine de Transport (AMT), ALDO, McAuslan, La Ville de Montréal, Le Ministère des Affaires Municipales, des Régions et de l'Occupation du Territoire (MAMROT), SODEC, Tourism Quebec and Tourism Montreal.

In an open press release, the band stated: "We thank all who have been integral in putting this event together. We thank them for supporting and continuing to support Canadian Independent Music."

SiriusXM Canada broadcasted the live concert exclusively throughout Canada and the broadcast was seen as a major breakthrough in a continuing quest to showcase Canada's most influential artists, especially in the US. At last, it seems, Canrock had gained major kudos in the US, largely due to the idiosyncratic nature of a major band like Arcade Fire.

As Régine stated, the show coincided with the French release of Tracy Kidder's book *Mountains Beyond Mountains (Soulever Les Montagnes)*, which documents the story of Paul Farmer, one of the founders of Partners In Health. For this show, the band offered a special deal: the first 100 people to make a $200+ donation to KANPE received two passes to the VIP area at the show and a copy of the book. KANPE is a Montreal-based partner organisation of Partners In Health that is dear to the band's heart. Its work seeks to reverse the cycle of poverty in Haiti by encouraging financial independence, and enabling every person to live healthily and with dignity.

The close of 2011 felt like the end of more than another year. Not that 2011 is ever likely to trouble 1968 or 1976 in terms of classic music or deeply embedded social poignancy. A great deal happened in 2011 although very little of it seemed linked to the often tepid, unsurprising and genre-clamped music that swirled around a media preoccupied with the multi-national nuances of televised talent shows featuring hopeful youngsters warbling cover versions of well-known hits.

But as Arcade Fire disengaged themselves from a three-year chunk of activity surrounding the writing, recording and promoting of *The Suburbs*, as they dived back into Montreal and went their separate ways, picking up lost musical threads here and there, seizing the opportunity to allow the demands of their phenomenal success to lessen, if only for a few months, it seemed like, for them at least, an era was collapsing perfectly. The kick-on effect of this success wouldn't allow them to completely divorce themselves from the commercial force – if they stopped completely, there and then, the momentum would still bubble away across the globe for many years.

However, if there is one band on earth that really are capable of falling back into some semblance of normal life, then that band might well be Arcade Fire. Their dilemma is a time-honoured rock problem, of course, and can be seen fully in the difference between Oasis' *Definitely*

Maybe – an album about feeling great while skint and dreaming of being rock stars – and *Be Here Now* – an uninspired album about the clichéd delights of actually being a rock star and positive proof, if proof were needed, that once fame is achieved there really is nothing there. Of course, Arcade Fire are no Oasis and their heads are less likely to be turned and dulled by the downside of blind adoration. Morrissey may thrive on this sort of thing but there is a fear in Win Butler's eyes that becomes apparent every time a fan begins to hover close. Of course, the fact that the entire band appear uncomfortable whenever musical success turns towards the fringe of celebrity is surely a saving grace. It is all the easier, therefore, to place that baggage on one side and search for a source of inspiration that appears organic, untainted by the demands of stardom. Mercifully, in Merge Records, Arcade Fire are blessed with a record company that understands the need for them to have space and time to mine for inspiration rather than bullishly demanding new product whenever a hiatus is met. Rough Trade also, by reputation if not always fact – Morrissey may argue his case here – prefers to be dictated to by the organic sway of the artist's muse. Well, to some extent, of course.

Jeremy Gara, to *The Irish Post*: "At this point, we have a huge collection of bits of songs, some more complete than others, and we'll just keep picking at them. The nice thing is – well, the nice thing for us, people might get annoyed – but it might take us three years to make a record, or it could take us three months. We really have no idea, but it sort of feels at this point that it could be quick this time, because we're all able to settle in at home and get creative quite quickly. So it'd be nice to just bang out a record and keep the momentum going."

A new creative space for the band is in the works too, he enthused. "We haven't touched those bits and pieces of songs for a few months, so we'll have to freshen them up a bit. But the nice thing is that by the time we play Electric Picnic and a couple more shows, we'll have a new studio space. It's being built here in Montreal at the moment, and we're really excited about playing music in it together. Because we're such a weird, big group that it's actually kind of a challenge to play music altogether and have it sound reasonable – so once we're done touring, we're gonna close the door and dive back in. And we'll see where it takes us."

However, at the close of 2011 it still seems difficult to locate exactly where Arcade Fire fit into the scheme of things at the top of rock's unholy hierarchy. It is not allowed, for example, for a band of their status to retain any sense of organic urgency while at the top of the tree. The accepted length of time between albums by top attractions seems to be at least two years and, the bigger you are, probably three. Indeed, the natural cycle is for a softening of all edges until an irksomely vacuous beast emerges to attain even greater commercial success than ever before. There are many who believe that, in producing *The Suburbs*, Arcade Fire achieved exactly this; a radio-friendly version of their former selves, where idiosyncracy was ironed out and the artist would succeed to a genre defined only by shallow success. While I strongly disagree that this is the case, I can understand the misconception. In November 2011 in, of all organs, *The Sunday Telegraph*, a rather lightweight and uninformed review of the new Snow Patrol album appeared to warn the band of the dangers of becoming another U2 or Arcade Fire. The notion that Arcade Fire had already planted their flag in this tepid arena was made all the more ludicrous by the reviewer's steely defence of Snow Patrol. While personal taste certainly enters into this and is difficult to argue against, it also proves the point. People *expect* a band of this magnitude to fall from artistic grace and to lose that initial spark.

The ideal scenario would be for Arcade Fire to somehow turn this end into a new beginning. That is where the true hope lies. While increasingly difficult in the modern world, it had been achieved many times before, most obviously through the artistic metamorphoses perfected by titans such as Bob Dylan, David Bowie, U2 and, less successfully, by Coldplay and Franz Ferdinand in more recent times. The contemporary commercial music world doesn't take kindly to unexpected change, especially when its skin is frazzled by recession. Furthermore, even if an artistic sea-change is warmly welcomed by the critics, it often fails to translate into gargantuan sales and increased success. Whether Arcade Fire like it or not, the bulk of their international audience remain sold on the sound they created for *The Suburbs* and their expectations remain within that area.

Then again, it is a dilemma that might even spur them to greater heights. What is certain – and comforting – is that, at the close of 2011, they have scattered into the shadows of some kind of normality where, hopefully, that muse will remain playful and unique.

Acknowledgements

Thanks to: Chris Charlesworth at Omnibus Press, Jacqui Black, Vicky Barlow, Paul Morley, John Doran, Luke Turner, John Robb, Lindsay Reade, Kathryn Turner, Spencer Turner, Vincent Moon, Spike Jonze, Dounia Mikou and all at the *Warrington Guardian*.

Also, the following websites: arcadefire.com, uskidsknow.com, www.kanpe.org, www.pih.org, pitchfork.com; and newspapers and magazines: *The Times, The Observer, Uncut, Mojo, Wire, R2, Rolling Stone, The Irish Times, New Musical Express, The Guardian, Independent.*

Concert Listing

2002
May
12 – Ottawa, ON – Zaphod Beeblebrox (with Jacob Earl & These Imperial Times and Gay As The Day Is Long)
16 – Montreal, QC – 1619 William Street (Loft Party)
28 – Montreal, QC – 1619 William Street (Loft Party)

December
1 – Montreal, QC – La Sala Rossa

2003
January
1 – Montreal, QC – La Sala Rossa (with the Hidden Cameras)
10 – Toronto, ON – El Mocambo (supporting Jim Guthrie, with Cryin' Out Loud Choir)

February
2 – Ottawa, ON – Babylon (opening for Clark)

March

29 – Montreal, QC – Casa Del Popolo – EP Release Party (with Parka 3, Big Gold Hoops, and Kosher Dill Spears)

April

12 – Montreal, QC – Jupiter Room (with Melon Galia and Wolf Parade)

June

10 – Montreal, QC – La Sala Rossa (with Royal City and Sufjan Stevens)

July

2 – Brantford, Ontario – The Ford Plant (with Nathan Lawr, The Majesties and Ryan Stanley)
3 – Toronto, Ontario – Rivoli (with Nathan Lawr)
5 – London, Ontario – The Office (with Nathan Lawr)
7 – Guelph, Ontario – The Black Mustard (with Nathan Lawr and Derek & The Sprayers)
10 – Cambridge – The Zeitgeist Gallery (with Devendra Banhart and Xiu Xiu)

September

6 – Ottawa – Barrymore's
9 – Montreal – La Sala Rossa (with Wolf Parade & Bell Orchestre)
11 – Guelph – Ed Video (with Wolf Parade, The Barmitzvah Brothers, and Cryin' Out Loud Choir)
13 – Toronto, ON – Rivoli (with The Barcelona Pavilion and Wolf Parade)
27 – Montreal, QC – Club Soda (opened for Phaser & Hawksley Workman)

October

11 – Toronto – The Horeshoe Tavern (with The Constantines and Jim Guthrie)

16 – Montreal – La Sala Rossa (supporting The Constantines)

2004
January
9 – Toronto – Sneaky Dee's (with The Barmitzvah Brothers and Spitfires & Mayflowers)
10 – Guelph – Ed Video (with The Barmitzvah Brothers)
11 – Hamilton – The Underground (with The Barmitzvah Brothers)
21 – Montreal – La Sala Rossa (with Wolf Parade and Belle Orchestre)

February
6 – Montreal, QC – Casa del Popolo (with The Wrens)
13 – Montreal, QC – Pavilion (with Hidden Cameras)

March
4 – Toronto, ON – 44 Sudbury (secret show for Canadian Music Week)
26 – New York, NY – The Knitting Factory (with The Wrens and Baby)

April
12 – New York, NY – The Knitting Factory (with The Unicorns and Chromeo)

May
6 – New York, NY – The Knitting Factory (with The Broken Spindles, Passage & Restiform Bodies)

June
(Full tour, supporting The Unicorns)
6 – Washington, DC – Black Cat (with Death From Above 1979)
7 – Columbia, SC – New Brookland Tavern
8 – Atlanta, GA – Echo Lounge
10 – Birmingham, AL – The Nick

11 – New Orleans, LA – One Eyed Jack's
12 – Houston, TX – Mary Jane's Fat Cat
14 – Austin, TX – Emo's (outside)
15 – Denton, TX – Hailey's
16 – Oklahoma City, OK – The Conservatory
17 – St. Louis, MO – Rocket Bar
18 – Chicago, IL – Open End Gallery
19 – Milwaukee, WI – Mad Planet (two shows)
21 – Pittsburgh, PA – Rex Theatre
22 – Rochester, NY – Bug Jar
23 – Toronto, ON – Lee's Palace (with Les Mouches)
27 – Montreal, QC – El Salon (with Les Mouches)

July
24 – Guelph, ON – Hillside Festival
28 – Chapel Hill, NC – Local 506 (with Lou Barlow)

August
7 – Toronto, ON – Toronto Island – Hot August Night (w/ Sloan, Broken Social Scene, Sam Roberts, The Stills, Constantines, Buck 65, and Death From Above 1979)

September
25 – Montreal, QC – The Salvation Army Citadel
26 – Wakefield, QC – Black Sheep Inn (with Hilotrons)
29 – Kingston, ON – Clark Hall Pub
30 – Guelph, ON – The Trasheteria (Club Vinyl) (with The Barmitzvah Brothers)

October
11 – Toronto, ON – Lee's Palace (with Bell Orchestre)
12 – Hamilton, Ontario – Underground
13 – New York , NY – Mercury Lounge (Merge CMJ Showcase)
14 – New York, NY – Museum of Television and Radio (KEXP 90.3 Live Performance)

16 – New York, NY – Arlene's Grocery – IAMSOUND and AAM CMJ Showcase (with Saturday Looks Good To Me, Q & Not U, and Sparta)
30 – Bar Harbor, ME – College of the Atlantic (Halloween Show)

November
5 – Halifax, NS, – The Marquee w/ The Organ
10 – Medford, MA – Hotung Cafe -Tufts U
11 – New York, NY – Bowery Ballroom (with The Hidden Cameras)
12 – Boston, MA – TT the Bear's (with The Hidden Cameras)
13 – Ithaca, NY – Cornell University – Noyes Community Center
14 – Philadelphia, PA – First Unitarian Church
15 – Pittsburgh, PA – Garfield Artworks
16 – Cleveland, OH – Beachland Ballroom
18 – Detroit, MI – Magic Stick
19 – Cincinnati, OH – Southgate House
20 – Lexington, KY – The Dame
21 – Champaign, IL – High Dive
23 – Iowa City, IA – Gabe's Oasis
24 – Milwaukee, WI – Mad Planet
25 – Chicago, IL – Logan Square Auditorium
26 – Chicago, IL – Empty Bottle
27 – Minneapolis, MN – 400 Bar (with Haley Bonar)
29 – Omaha, NE – Sokol Underground (with Kite Pilot)
30 – Columbia, MO – Mojo's

December
1 – Lawrence, KS – Jackpot Saloon
3 – Denver, CO – Larimer Lounge
6 – Phoenix, AZ – Modified Arts (with Sweetbleeders)
7 – Los Angeles, CA – Spaceland
8 – San Francisco, CA – Bottom of the Hill
10 – Portland, OR – Bossanova Ballroom (with Fembots, Murder by Death, The Weakerthans)
11 – Seattle, WA – Neumos

177

12 – Vancouver, BC – Commodore Ballroom   12/13 Victoria, BC –
Lucky Bar
14 – Vancouver, BC – Mesa Luna

2005
January
12-14 – San Francisco, CA – Great American Music Hall
15/16 – Los Angeles, CA – Troubadour
17 – San Diego, CA – The Casbah
18 – Tucson, AZ – Solar Culture
21 – Austin, TX – Emo's
22 – Dallas, TX – Trees
23 – Houston, TX – Fat Cat's
24 – New Orleans, LA – The Parish Room
26 – Atlanta, GA – Variety Playhouse
27 – Asheville, NC – The Orange Peel
28 – Carrboro, NC – Cat's Cradle
30 – Washington, DC, – 9:30 Club
31 – Philadelphia, PA – Theatre of Living Arts

February
1 – New York, NY – Webster Hall
2 – New York, NY – Irving Plaza
3 – Boston, MA – Roxy
8 – London, England – King's College
10 – Paris, France – Le Nouveau Casino
11 – Amsterdam, Netherlands – Melkweg (with Benjamin Winter)
13 – Berlin, Germany – Magnet
14 – Oslo, Norway – Garage
15 – Stockholm, Sweden – Debaser
17 – London, England – ULU

April
23-25 – Montreal, QC – Theatre Corona

26-28 – Toronto, ON – Danforth Music Hall

May
1 – Indio, CA – Empire Polo Field – Coachella Music Festival
4 – Manchester, England – Manchester University
5 – Glasgow, Scotland – Union Debating Chamber
6 – Birmingham, England – Carling Academy Birmingham
8 – Bristol, England – Carling Academy Bristol
9 – London, England – Astoria
11 – Amsterdam, Netherlands – Paradiso
12 – Rotterdam, Netherlands – Nighttown
14 – Tourcoing, France – Le Grand Mix (Cancelled)
15 – Brussels, Belgium – Cirque Royal
16 – Paris, France – Elysée-Montmartre
17 – Koln, Germany – Gebäude 9
18 – Hamburg, Germany – Knust
20 – Berlin, Germany – Postbahnhof
21 – Vienna, Austria – Flex
22 – Munich, Germany – Feierwerk
23 – Zurich, Switzerland – The Mascotte
24 – Milan, Italy – Rainbow
26 – Barcelona, Spain – Primavera Sound Festival
28 – George, WA – Sasquatch Music Festival – The Gorge Amphitheatre
26 – Hollywood, CA – KCRW World Music Series – The Hollywood Bowl (opening for David Byrne)

July
23 – Guelph, ON – Hillside Festival
24 – Grant Park, Chicago, IL – Lollapalooza

August
13 – Tokyo, Japan – Summersonic Festival
14 – Osaka, Japan – Summersonic Festival
17 – Paredes de Coura, Portugal – Festival Paredes de Coura

19 – Hasselt, Belgium – Pukkelpop Festival
20 – Biddinghuizen, Holland – Lowlands Festival
22 – Nantes, France – Olympic
25 – Paris, France – Rock En Seine Festival
26 – Koln, Germany – Monsters of Spex
27 – Reading, England – Reading Festival
28 – Leeds, England – Leeds Festival
30 – Liverpool, England – Carling Academy
31 – Edinburgh, Scotland – Princes Street Gardens (opening for Franz Ferdinand)

September
1 – Sheffield, England – Sheffield Leadmill
3 – Stradbally, Ireland – Electric Picnic
Fall Tour (opening acts: Wolf Parade & Bell Orchestre)
8 – New York, NY – Fashion Rocks – Radio City Music Hall
15 – New York, NY – Summerstage – Central Park (with Sound Team & Bell Orchestre)
17 – Devore, CA – KROQ Inland Invasion 5 – Glen Helen Hyundai Pavilion
18 – San Francisco, CA – The Warfield
20 – Portland, OR – Crystal Ballroom
21 – Seattle, WA – The Paramount
23 – Austin, TX – Stubb's BBQ (w/ The Black Keys)
25 – Austin, TX – Austin City Limits – Zilker Park
28 – Chicago, IL – Riviera Theatre
29 – Minneaplis, MN – First Avenue
30 – Winnipeg, MB – Burton Cummings Theatre

October
2 – Saskatoon, SK – Odeon Event Center
4 – Edmonton, AB – Red's
5 – Calgary, AB – MacEwan Hall
7 – Vancouver, BC – PNE Forum
8 – Mountain View, CA – Download Festival – Shoreline Amphitheatre

22 – Rio de Janeiro, Brazil – Tim Festival – Museu de Arte Moderna
23 – Sao Paulo, Brazil – Tim Festival – Arena Skol Anhembi
25 – Porto Alegre, Brazil – Tim Festival – Pavilhão (Aeroporto)
30 – Las Vegas, NV –Vegoose – Sam Boyd Stadium

November
Opening For U2
25 Ottawa, ON – Corel Centre
26/28 Montreal, QC – Bell Centre

2006
No shows played.

2007
January
19 – Ottawa, ON – Canterbury High School
20 – Montreal, QC – St. Michael Catholic Church
29-31 London, England – St John's Church, Smith Square

February
1/2 – London, England – Porchester Hall
6-9 Montreal, QC – Ukrainian National Federation
13-17 – New York, NY – Judson Memorial Church

March
European Tour (opening acts: Patrick Wolf 03/05 – 03/15, Electrelane 03/16 – 04/05)
5/6 – Dublin, Ireland – Olympia
8/9 – Manchester, England – Apollo
11/12 Glasgow, Scotland – Barrowlands
14-17 – London, England – Brixton Academy
19/20 – Paris, France – Olympia
23 – Stockholm, Sweden – Cirkus

24 – Oslo, Norway – Centrum Scene (cancelled due to illness)
25 – Copenhagen, Denmark – KB Hallen (cancelled)
27 – Berlin, Germany – Postbahnhof (cancelled)
28- Munich, Germany – Elserhalle (cancelled)
31 – Lyon, France – Transbordeur (cancelled)

April
1 – Cologne, Germany – Palladium (cancelled)
2 – Utrecht, Netherlands – Vredenburg (cancelled)
4- Brussels, Belgium – Halles de Schaerbeek (cancelled)
5 – Lille, France – L'Aéronef (cancelled)
26 – San Diego, CA – Spreckels Theatre (with Cass McCombs)
28 – Indio, CA – Empire Polo Field (Coachella)

May
1 – Atlanta, GA – Civic Center (with The National)
2 – Asheville, NC – Thomas Wolfe Auditorium (with The National)
4 – Washington, DC – DAR Constitution Hall (with The National)
5 – Philadelphia, PA – Tower Theatre (with The National)
7-9 – New York, NY – The United Palace (with The National)
10 – Boston, MA – Orpheum Theatre (with Wild Light)
12/13 – Montreal, Quebec – Arena Maurice Richard (with St. Vincent)
15/16 – Toronto, Ontario – Massey Hall (with Handsome Furs)
18-20 – Chicago, IL – Chicago Theatre (with St. Vincent)
24 – Burnaby, BC – Deer Lake Park (with St. Vincent)
26 – George, WA – The Gorge – Sasquatch Festival
27 – Portland, OR – Schnitzer Concert Hall (with Electrelane)
29/30 – Los Angeles, CA – Greek Theatre (with Electrelane)

June
1/2 – Berkeley, CA – Greek Theatre (with Electrelane)
22 – Glastonbury Festival, England
23 – Scheeßel, Germany – Hurricane Festival
24 – Tuttlingen, Germany – Southside Festival

27 – Arendal, Norway (Tromøy) – Hovefestivalen
30 – St Gallen, Switzerland – Open Air St Gallen

July
1 – Belfort, France – Les Eurockéennes
3 – Lisbon, Portugal – Super Bock Super Rock
5 – Roskilde, Denmark – Roskilde Festival
7 – Kinross, Scotland – Balado Park – T In The Park
8 – Ireland – Oxegen Festival
11 – Ferrara, Italy – Piazza Castello – Bands Apart Festival
13 – Parc del Fòrum, Barcelona, Spain – Summercase Festival
14 – Viñas Viejas, Boadilla del Monte – Madrid, Spain – Summercase Festival
15 – Southwold, Suffolk, UK – Henham Park – Latitude Festival
18 – Lyon, France – Les Nuits de Fourvière
20 – Carhaix, France – Festival des Vieilles Charrues
21 – Angoulême, France – Garden Nef Party
22 – Nimes, France – Festival de Nimes
25 – Nyon, Switzerland – Paleo Festival

August
17 – Hasselt, Belgium – Pukkelpop Festival
19 – Biddinghuizen, Holland – Lowlands Festival
22 – Cologne, Germany – Palladium
24 – Paris, France – Rock En Seine
25 – Reading, England – Reading Festival
26 – Leeds, England – Leeds Festival

September
15 – Austin, TX – Austin City Limits Festival
17 – Denver, CO – Red Rocks Amphitheatre
20 – Los Angeles, CA – Hollywood Bowl (with Wild Light)
21 – Mountain View, CA – Shoreline Amphitheatre
24 – Seattle, WA – Bank of America Arena
26 – Lehi, UT – Thanksgiving Point

28- Kansas City, MO – Starlight Theatre
30 – St Paul, MN – Roy Wilkins Auditorium

October
3 – Louisville, KY – Waterfront Park
5 – Columbus, OH – LC Pavilion
6 – New York, NY – Randall's Island (with Blonde Redhead, Les Savy Fav and Wild Light)
23/24 Dublin, Ireland – Phoenix Park (with Clinic)
26 – Glasgow, Scotland – SECC (with Clinic)
27 – Manchester, England – MEN Arena (with Clinic)
29 – Newcastle, England – Metro Radio Arena (with Clinic)
30 – Cardiff, Wales – International Arena (also with Clinic)
31 – Nottingham, England – Arena (with Clinic)

November
2 – Brussels, Belgium – Forest National
4 – Oslo, Norway – Spektrum
5 – Stockholm, Sweden – Annexet
7 – Copenhagen, Denmark – KB Hallen
9 – Berlin, Germany – Columbiahalle
10 – Vienna, Austria – Gasometer
11 – Munich, Germany – Tonhalle
13 – Amsterdam, The Netherlands – Heineken Music Hall
17-19 – London, England – Alexandra Palace (with Clinic)

2008
January
18 – Auckland, New Zealand – Mt Smart Stadium (Big Day Out)
20- Gold Coast, Australia – Parklands (Big Day Out)
22/23 – Sydney, Australia – Enmore Theatre (with Spoon)
25 – Sydney, Australia – Showground (Big Day Out)
28 – Melbourne, Australia – Flemington Racecourse (Big Day Out)
29/30 – Melbourne, Australia – Forum Theatre (with Spoon)

February
1 – Adelaide, Australia – Showground (Big Day Out)
3 – Perth, Australia – Claremont Showground (Big Day Out)
7 – Osaka, Japan – Namba Hatch
8 – Nagoya, Japan – Diamond Hall
11 – Tokyo, Japan – Studio Coast

March
Barack Obama Campaign Shows
2 – Nelsonville, OH – Stuart's Operat House (two shows)
3 – Cleveland, OH – Beachland Ballroom (two shows)

2009
No shows played.

2010
June
7/8 – Sherbrooke, QC – Théâtre Granada
9 – Longueuil, QC – Place Longueuil parking lot
11/12 – Toronto, ON – Danforth Music Hall
28 – Helsinki – Senaatintori Finland
30 – Rättvik Dalhalla – Sweden

July
2 – Arendal Hove Festival – Norway
4 – Werchter Rock Werchter – Belgium
5 – Paris Casino de Paris – France
7 – London Hackney Empire – United Kingdom
9 – Punchestown Oxegen – Ireland
12 – Québec Festival d'été de Québec
13 – Ottawa – Ottawa Bluesfest
31 – Montreal – Osheaga

2011
April
10 – Broomfield, CO – 1st Bank Center
11 – Orem, UT – The UCCU Center
13 – Phoenix, AZ – Comerica Theatre
14 – Las Vegas, NV – The Joint at Hard Rock Hotel
16 – Indio, CA – Coachella
18 – Santa Fe, NM – Santa Fe Convention Center
20 – Kansas City, MO – Starlight Amphitheatre
22-25 – Chicago, IL – UIC Pavilion
27 – Indianapolis, IN – The Lawn at White River State Park
28 – Memphis, TN – Orpheum Theatre
30 – Dallas, TX – Gexa Energy Pavilion

May
3 – Austin, TX – The Backyard
4 – The Woodlands, TX – Cynthia Woods Mitchell Pavilion
6 – New Orleans, LA – Jazz and Heritage Festival

June
17 – Scheebel Hurricane Festival – Germany
18 – Neuhausen ob Eck Southside Festival – Germany
21 – Zagreb T-Mobile Festival – Croatia
22 – Wiesen, Austria – Festivalgelande
26 – Roeser, Luxemburg – Rock A Field Festival
30 – Hyde Park, London (with Mumford & Sons, The Vaccines, Beirut)

July
2 – Arras, France. Main Square Festival (with Kaiser Chiefs, Kasabian, Coldplay)
3 – Belfort, France, Les Eurockéenes de Belfort
5 – Milan. Milano Jazz Festival – Italy
7 – Novo Sad Exit Festival – Serbia.
9 – Lucca Summer Festival – Italy
12 – Argeles-sur-Mer Les Déferlantes Festival – France

13 – Guggenheim Bilbao – Spain
15 – Lisbon – Super Bock Super Rock
17 – Benicassim Festival – Spain
30 – Moncton Magnestic Hill Festival – Canada

August
31 – Manchester – MEN Arena

September
1 – Edinburgh Castle. Scotland

Discography

Funeral

Neighborhood #1 (Tunnels), Neighborhood #2 (Laika), Une
Année Sans Lumiere (Translated), Neighborhood #3 (Power Out),
Neighborhood #4 (7 Kettles), Crown Of Love, Wake Up Haiti
(Translated), Rebellion (Lies), In The Backseat
CD released in the US on Merge Records on September 14,
2004 (MRG255)
CD released in Australia on Spunk Records on February 7,
2005 (URA 141)
12" Vinyl LP released in the US on Merge Records on February 22,
2005 (MRG255)
CD released in the UK on Rough Trade on February 28,
2005 (RTRADCD219)
12" Vinyl LP released in the UK on Rough Trade on February 28,
2005 (RTRADLP219)
CD released in Japan on V2 Records on July 20, 2005 (V2CP228)

Arcade Fire EP
Old Flame, I'm Sleeping In A Submarine, No Cars Go, The Woodland National Anthem, My Heart Is An Apple, Headlights Look Like Diamonds, Vampires / Forest Fire
CD EP self-released in 2003
Remastered EP re-issued on Rough Trade (UK) on June 13, 2005 (RTRADCD248)
Remastered EP re-issued on Merge Records (US) on July 12, 2005 (MRG269)
Also commonly referred to as *Us Kids Know*. The initial run had slightly different packaging, and a newer version was available at shows. Merge & Rough Trade both re-issued remastered & repackaged versions of the EP in the summer of 2005.

Neon Bible
Black Mirror, Keep The Car Running, Neon Bible, Intervention, Black Wave / Bad Vibrations, Ocean of Noise, The Well And The Lighthouse, (Antichrist Television Blues), Windowsill, No Cars Go, My Body Is A Cage
CD released by Merge Records on March 6, 2007 (MRG285)
Deluxe CD released by Merge Records on March 6, 2007 (MRG300)
12" Vinyl LP released by Merge Records on March 8, 2007 (MRG285)

The Suburbs
The Suburbs, Ready to Start, Modern Man, Rococo, Empty Room, City With No Children, Half Light I, Half Light II (No Celebration), Suburban War, Month Of May, Wasted Hours, Deep Blue, We Used To Wait, Sprawl I (Flatland), Sprawl II (Mountains Beyond Mountains), The Suburbs (continued)
CD released by Merge Records on August 3rd, 2010 (MRG385)
12" Vinyl released by Merge Records on August 3rd, 2010 (MRG385)

Cover Versions

The background and influence of music on Arcade Fire is vividly reflected by the ever-increasing number of cover versions they perform live. Indeed, their delight in performing impromptu and unexpected covers has become legendary over the years and the collection contains a number of surprises.

One can imagine them one day releasing an astonishing Arcade Fire covers album which would certainly be no mere contract filler. Indeed, the very act of imposing their live power on some lonely and often forgotten track, plucked from Win's record collection, perhaps, is as fascinating as the aura that surrounds them. At times – the performing of 'Born In The USA' at the Barack Obama Staff Ball, for instance – they are merely obvious reflections of the mood of the moment. Elsewhere, however, songs by others stir up enthusiasm between the seven musicians as they shuffle their iPods on the tour bus, with each band member seeking to find a distinctive place in any given number.

This love of cover versions reflects back to those early seventies offshoot releases by David Bowie (*Pin Ups*) and Bryan Ferry (*These Foolish Things*). Those two key covers albums helped define a genre that has had a somewhat chequered history in the intervening years. But there are few contemporary bands, I suggest, whose choice of cover can seem so indefinable and disparate.

Here is a by no means complete – who knows what they may have sung in those early house party gigs? – run-through of songs performed on the Arcade Fire stage during the past six years:
'A Change Is Gonna Come' (Sam Cooke)
'Age Of Consent' (New Order)
'All The Umbrellas In London' (Magnetic Fields)
'Born In The USA' (Bruce Springsteen)
'Born On A Train' (Magnetic Fields)
'Brazil' (Ary Barroso & Ed Russell)
'Distortions' (Clinic)
'Five Years' (David Bowie)
'Gimme Some Truth' (John Lennon)

'Girls Just Wanna Have Fun' (Cyndi Lauper)
'Guns Of Brixton' (The Clash)
'Helpless' (Neil Young)
'Kiss Off' (Violent Femmes)
'The Last Time' (The Rolling Stones)
'Maps' (Yeah Yeah Yeahs)
'Heroes' (David Bowie)
'Poupée de Cire, Poupée de Son' (France Gall)
'Still Ill' (The Smiths)
'State Trooper' (Bruce Springsteen)
'Such A Shame' (Jay Reatard)
'This Must Be The Place (Naive Melody)' (Talking Heads)
'Wave Of Mutilation' (Pixies)
'Boys Don't Cry' (The Cure)
'Love Will Tear Us Apart' (Joy Division)
'Bizarre Love Triangle' (New Order)
'Dancing In The Dark' (Bruce Springsteen)

This hardly comprehensive list would make a perfect MP3 collection (called *Avenues Of Influence*, perhaps?) and certainly showcases some of the many twists and turns in their music. Of particular interest is the rendition of 'Helpless', performed with Neil Young himself in October 2011 at the Bridge School Benefit Concert, Mountain View, California. It was the first occasion that Young had joined the band on stage for an all-Canadian collaboration that strongly reflected the moment when Young performed the same beautiful song with The Band, as captured in Martin Scorsese's *The Last Waltz*.